GOOD LIFE

GOOD LIFE

Reflections on what we value today

_____

NIGEL BIGGAR

First published in Great Britain 1997
Society for Promoting Christian Knowledge
Holy Trinity Church
Marylebone Road
London
NW1 4DU

Biblical quotations are from *The Revised Standard Version
of the Bible* (c) 1971 and 1952.

British Library Cataloguing in Publication Data

A catalogue record for this book is available
from the British Library.

ISBN 0-281-05023-6

Typeset by Pioneer Associates, Perthshire
Printed in Great Britain by
The Cromwell Press, Melksham, Wiltshire

CONTENTS

Acknowledgements vii

Preface ix

1 JUST A MATTER OF TASTE?
The question of moral relativism 1

2 SELF-FULFILMENT
. . . must it be selfish? 15

3 FREEDOM
. . . for what? 30

4 WORK
. . . on not making a tyranny out of a necessity ... 46

5 ECSTASY
. . . rising up, moving out, and connecting 57

6 TRIBAL LOYALTY
. . . caring for the tribe by looking beyond it 71

7 TOLERANCE
. . . not indifference 84

8 COMMUNITY
. . . how can we build it? 93

9 TO WHOM SHALL WE TURN?
The questions of moral education and authority ... 130

Notes 143

Further Reading 161

Index 163

ACKNOWLEDGEMENTS

In the course of writing this book, I have benefited greatly from the solicited advice and the unsolicited encouragement of many people, and I gladly record my debt of gratitude to them.

In particular I would like to mention: Dr David Attwood; Ginny Biggar; Rufus Black; Laurence Cranmer; Andrew Dilnot; Professor Arthur Francis; Dr Harriet Harris; Dr Keith Hawkins; Jeremy and Katie Hill; Simon Laver; the Rev. Mike Lloyd; Nick McDowell; the Rev. Helena Lady Mackinnon; Dr David Maxwell; the members of the Civil Service College course, 'Management through People', held at Manchester College, Oxford, in April 1995; the Rev. Mike O'Connor; Dr Mark Philp; Chris Roberts; Marc Teasdale; Wendy Robinson; Nick Townsend; Simon Walters; Ben Webster; and Joanne Woolway.

I owe special thanks to Brendan Walsh who, as Managing Editor of SPCK, was enthusiastic in commissioning me to write; and to the Trustees of the St Augustine's Foundation who funded me as I did so.

Nigel Biggar
Oriel College, Oxford

PREFACE

This book risks being patronizing.

In it I want to talk about what we value today. I want to identify and reflect upon some of the things we tend to build our lives around, some of the things we are wont to invest ourselves in. I try to fit myself into the shoes of the reader, to take a few steps back from the daily business of keeping the show of life more or less on the road, and to think not only about movement but about direction. About destination.

But which pair of shoes? Which reader? Surely there are many different individuals or groups of individuals, each of whom holds a different set of values? So isn't talk about 'we' patronizing, treating everyone as if they could be squeezed into a single mould, one constructed by me out of my own limited personal and social experience?

The danger of trying to write about what 'we' value today was brought home to me at a wedding reception. 'And what do you do?' asked a schoolteacher. 'Among other things,' I replied, 'I write books.' 'What kind of books?' she enquired. 'Well, for example,' I said, 'I'm currently planning to write one on contemporary values, on the kinds of things people construct their lives around these days.' 'But who's going to read that?' retorted her neighbour, an unemployed actor. 'Most of us are far too busy just trying to make ends meet to have the leisure to sit back and muse about what we value. Twice I've been in the position of not being able to pay my bills, and I was absolutely terrified. So the driving force in my life ever since has been simply to make damn sure I never find myself in that place again.'

Discreetly, I gulped.

For, even though having enough money to pay the bills is itself a value, and even though this is a value because it serves other values such as the preservation of life, the possession of freedom, and participation in community, these words are nevertheless sobering. They are sobering for someone like me who aspires to talk about what 'we' value, and yet has always been able to take a comfortable level of economic security for granted. For it reminds me that those whom I have sought first to understand and then to address, are not 'everyone'. And it warns me that some of those who read this book, and find themselves embraced by the authorial 'we', might well feel ill-represented.

So in order to prevent misunderstanding, let me make clear, here at the beginning, who it is that I have imagined myself talking to in the course of writing. Generally, my typical conversation partners live in a liberal western society, and they tend to embrace western culture in its late-twentieth century form. Occasionally, they are specifically British. Whether or not they tend to be middle class, I am not sure; but I would not be surprised to learn that they do. Certainly, they do not necessarily regard themselves as religious.

This, then, is who 'we' are in this book; and it is (some of) the moral assumptions and values of such people that I have sought to identify, understand and reflect upon.

Finally, a word about the organization of this book. Its chapters are not stages in a single argument that runs from the first page through to a conclusion in the last. Each chapter deals with a discrete topic, whether a general question (Chapters One and Nine) or particular values (Chapters Two to Eight); and although the topics are related and sometimes interrelated, and although there is a loose logic to their sequence, each chapter is largely designed to be read independently of the others. The coherence of the book derives, then, not so much from a strict linear structure, as from the constancy of the perspective within which the various topics are viewed.

1

JUST A MATTER OF TASTE?
THE QUESTION OF
MORAL RELATIVISM

> The true believer is the real danger. The study of history and
> culture teaches that all the world was mad in the past; men
> always thought they were right, and that led to wars, persecu-
> tions, slavery, xenophobia, racism, and chauvinism. The point
> is not to correct the mistakes and really be right; rather it is not
> to think you are right at all.[1]

The tone is ironic. The subject-matter is the outlook of today's
typical American undergraduate. The author is Allan Bloom,
writing in his controversial best-seller, *The Closing of the
American Mind*. In this critique of the prevalent ethos of university education, Bloom laments the moral relativism that has
become the unquestionable faith of contemporary students.
Challenges to this faith in the form of claims that there are
moral truths that are true for everyone, are met, he reports,
with wide-eyed incomprehension. Anyone who dares to make
such claims is indignantly branded an absolutist and reckoned
among the witchhunters and ayatollahs. Intolerance is the only
vice recognized, and an undiscriminating openness to different
'value-systems' the only virtue.

What Bloom sees in today's American students is also visible
in their British counterparts: on the eastern side of the Atlantic
moral relativism rules pretty much OK, too. The distinction
between making a judgement and being judgemental is rarely
noticed. Moral values and convictions are usually assumed to

1

be fit not so much for thinking about as for feeling. They are regarded more as matters of taste than of reason; and, of course, for taste there's no accounting. And if no accounting, then no criticizing.

The world of students, however, is not the whole world. What holds among people who are somewhat artificially abstracted from the normal nexus of social ties and roles and responsibilities does not necessarily hold among others. Students, perhaps, can afford moral relativism more easily than those who are more firmly rooted in relationships where others depend on them and they on others – more easily, for example, than employers, spouses or parents.

Still, it is clear enough that relativism is not monopolized by students. How frequently we hear, whether in personal conversation or on TV or radio chat-shows, a statement of moral conviction emasculated by the preface, 'Well, speaking *personally* . . .' – meaning: 'What I am about to say is merely my own private opinion, which does not presume to make any claim at all on anybody else.' And how often a discussion of moral matters degenerates into an anodyne exchange of 'perspectives', involving statements of 'what's true *for me*' and comments of, 'Well, that's *different*' (as distinct from being either right or wrong!). It seems that many of us, and not just students, are inclined to regard morality as a matter of irreducibly private taste. Our emphasis falls instinctively on the relativity of morality.

But why?

The answer lies in a complex of interacting factors. In part, our usual emphasis can be attributed to our heightened awareness of the empirical diversity of morals. Modern means of communication, together with the development of societies that incorporate a plurality of races and cultures, expose us as never before to the fact that what *we* assume, morally speaking, is not always what *they* assume. It is clear that morals do vary according to place and time. This makes it harder for us to maintain that our own are eternally and universally true. Indeed, it encourages us to doubt whether truth has got much to do with the matter at all, and to suspect that we have the morals we do simply because of the accidents of culture.

Our retreat into cultural relativism in the face of moral diversity is accelerated by a general lack of confidence about asserting moral convictions. To some extent this is a symptom of post-imperial guilt. Acutely aware of the arrogance and ignorance with which our colonial forebears sometimes judged and interfered with the morals of 'native' peoples, we feel that we have altogether lost the right to make critical comment on the moral beliefs and practices of other cultures.

But our diffidence has a far deeper source than this. It lies in scepticism about the very possibility of moral knowledge. Before the modern era, which began to acquire some of its definitive features in the seventeenth century, there was a more widespread confidence in the existence of metaphysical or spiritual realities such as God and values, and in the possibility of knowing them. Because of this, it was then common to refer to theology and ethics as 'sciences'. In the modern world, however, such talk has come to seem nonsense. The title of 'science' is now reserved for the study of physical or 'natural' reality according to rigorous experimental methods; and derivatively for those forms of study of human and social behaviour that take the natural sciences as their model. Whatever conclusions are arrived at by means of modern scientific method are reckoned to deserve the full status of real, objective knowledge. Anything else – such as religious or moral belief – tends to be classified as 'mere' imagination or speculation or opinion or sentiment or taste. It cannot seriously claim to have a grip on reality, to refer to any real object. At best, such belief is expressive of the one who holds it. In other words, it is simply relative to the individual subject.[2]

This subjectivist form of moral relativism, however, is not just something that a dominant materialist philosophy has foisted on us. It is also something that positively attracts us. This is because it legitimates our intuition that genuine morality is not simply a matter of obeying the rules imposed on us by society. It's more personal than that, and in two respects. First, in that what is morally right is so, ultimately, because it helps to fulfil us as human persons; and second, in that any accurate discernment of our moral duty must be careful to take due account of the particular, and often messy, circumstances of

3

our lives. To some extent, then, moral subjectivism is a reaction against an authoritarian morality that has been so concerned to uphold the authority of moral laws as to have lost sight of what they are designed to achieve, and of how to interpret them with sensitivity.

Not that the motives that move us to embrace subjectivism are always so reasonable. Sometimes they seem to be part of what has been called 'a general retreat from each other of individuals in modern society, a more or less deliberate self-protective policy of drifting apart'.[3] We want to be autonomous and self-determining, not because the moral authorities in our lives have been particularly careless and unfeeling, but because we simply do not want to be told what to do. We do not want to be accountable to other people. We do not want our style to be cramped.

Our penchant for moral relativism, then, is the product of a combination of factors: awareness of moral diversity, post-imperial guilt, diffidence about the possibility of moral knowledge, opposition to legalism, and wilful individualism. Elements of several of these factors deserve credit. But the position to which we suppose they lead us as a whole, is rather confused. And it casts some very dark shadows.

When we claim that morals are relative, what do we actually mean? Do we mean to say that they are relative to culture? And do we mean by this that each culture has an idiosyncratic morality that is 'true' for it alone? And are we saying, then, that members of a given culture should not criticize conventional morality? Or are we saying only that each culture's morality has a right to immunity from judgement by outsiders – such that, for example, China is quite correct to fend off western complaints about its record on human rights by asserting that 'there are no absolute individual rights and freedoms'?[4] But why should another culture's morals be immune from our criticism? Is it because they are perfect and cannot be corrected and improved? But that implies that we have made a judgement about them, albeit a positive one. And do we really mean to extend this right indiscriminately to all cultures and their moralities? Not only to the tribesmen of Papua New Guinea or the pygmies of Central Africa, but also to the Branch Davidians of Waco, to the Mafiosi, and to the Khmers Rouges?

However, in claiming that morals are relative, perhaps we mean that they are subjective? If so, are we merely saying that what is right in a particular situation depends to some extent on its circumstances, including the subjectivity of the persons involved – for example their motives and intentions? Or are we saying something far stronger; namely, that morality is entirely invented by each individual? That its only basis lies in the individual's will?

If we mean the latter, and mean it seriously, then there are a number of rather grim implications that we will have to embrace. One of them is this: that, if moral values and principles have no ultimate grounding in an objective reality that transcends the individual will, if they are really just arbitrary fictions, then human action is drained of much of its significance. It loses all moral weight. No longer have we reason to dignify what we do with the title of 'right' or 'just', for now we know that these words really say nothing more than 'willed'. No longer can we structure our lives with the meaning of a moral adventure, an adventure whose success or failure turns upon our responses to the call to grow up and grow out in virtue, to become people who shine with such qualities as honesty, courage, patience, kindness and generosity. No longer can we continue to admire those who suffer in order to maintain their moral integrity in the face of great temptation, or to uphold justice against terrible oppression, or merely to tell the truth in contradiction of some great and ruthless lie. No longer can martyrdom in the cause of human rights make sense to us. Henceforth, we must face the brutal fact that we live in a moral wasteland, a moral void, where all that matters is prolonging pleasure and avoiding pain, and securing the power to do as much of both as possible. If moral values have no reality outside of the individual's will, if they are not at least as real as stones, then human action and human lives may not lose all of their significance; but they will lose all of their *humane* significance.

Further, if morality lacks grounding in objective reality, then appeals to justice will carry no more weight than expressions of mere distaste. If moral values are not real, then when I spontaneously react to some injury by exclaiming, 'That's not fair!', all that I have succeeded in doing is uttering a sophisticated – or, rather, a verbose – form of 'Ouch!' My response has all the force of a merely personal dislike.

Further still, if morality is just an arbitrary fiction, then human relations are reducible to a brutish struggle for power. In the course of the history of philosophy this cynical conclusion has been reached on several occasions. In Greece, five centuries before the birth of Christ, the Sophists held that morality was nothing but a social convention invented by the strong to control the weak. Almost two-and-a-half millennia later Karl Marx effectively reproduced the Sophist position when he argued that morality was nothing but a bourgeois tool for keeping the proletariat in its subordinate place. Shortly afterward, this argument was given a new twist when, in fierce reaction against what he saw as the enfeebling nature of Christianity, Friedrich Nietzsche proposed that morality should rather be understood as the means by which the (Christian) weak tie down the (heroic pagan) strong. But whoever is seen as doing the manipulating and being manipulated, in all these views morality is the tool of manipulation. It ends up being nothing other than an idealistic fiction deliberately propagated and exploited to control other people. Morality becomes a politically useful illusion, an instrument of the sheer will-to-power.

If this is the case, then not only do human relations become a deeply grim affair, but the prospects of resolving moral disagreements by peaceful means disappear from sight; for there remains no longer any hope of *rational* discussion about moral matters. Since there is no moral reality to know, moral opinions cannot claim to know it. They can therefore be neither true nor false. So when moral opinions clash, the conflict cannot be resolved by an appeal to reason. It can only be resolved by the triumph of one will over another – that is, by the triumph of superior might.

What we mean by moral relativism is often unclear. And when it becomes clearer, what it implies is deeply depressing –

at least for those who care about the quality of human life. So if we do care, and if we have no vested interest in remaining inconsistent, then it would seem to be time for us to do some rethinking. It would seem to be time for us to reconsider the reasons that have led us to a point of view so confused and so subversive of human dignity.

We need to think again about the diversity of morals among cultures, and about what it implies. We need to consider that it does not necessarily imply that moralities are *simply* the products of different material conditions and social arrangements, and have no grounding whatsoever in a universal moral reality. Suppose, for example, that an affluent western society with ample resources to maintain a prison system takes it for granted that the infliction of capital punishment on habitually violent criminals is cruel and abhorrent; whereas a society in the developing world that has no other means of protecting innocent citizens regards such punishment as just.[5] Here is a case where different economic circumstances occasion different moral judgements about the same practice. But that does not mean that morality is reducible to economics. Both societies employ irreducibly moral concepts such as the duty of government to defend innocent citizens against criminal injury, and some notion of what makes the punishment of criminals just. Economic conditions do not of themselves sprout these moral concepts. They do, however, shape their application. For when we bring concepts of political duty or criminal justice to bear upon a particular situation, when we ask, 'How can the Government best defend us against this kind of criminal injury?' or 'In what practices should the just punishment of violent criminals be realized?', the answers to these questions are bound to interpret those moral concepts with reference to prevailing circumstances, economic conditions included. But that does not mean that political duty and criminal justice are *merely* about economics.

So we need to reconsider the common assumption that the diversity of morals between cultures implies that morality is simply or absolutely determined by socio-economic factors. We also need to reconsider whether moral diversity between or within cultures is really so great as we tend to think, and whether it really supports the claim that there is no universal basis of morality that transcends particular cultures and individuals. You and I may disagree strongly and in principle about the morality of abortion, experimentation on human embryos, the legalization of euthanasia, UN military intervention in civil wars, and much else besides. Nevertheless, the probability is that we agree that murder is wrong, as is the harmful use of human beings without their consent. We might have different opinions about the morality of homosexual sex, but we probably find common ground in the affirmation that sex should properly take place only within relationships of love – and by love we probably mean not just infatuation, but care. The point is this: we can disagree at a specific level while agreeing at another more general one. We can disagree about a rule – that sex should be confined to heterosexual relationships – while agreeing about a related principle – that sex should be expressive of love – and about a related and intrinsic value – friendship. So, diversity does not necessarily exclude universality. As one contemporary philosopher puts it: 'Crudely, table manners differ – but all human kinds have table manners; marital arrangements differ – but all human kinds have marriages, and also have adulteries . . .'[6]

Moreover, if we are prepared to engage with one another, instead of retreating into allegedly 'private' worlds; and if we are prepared to exercise the virtues of, say, courage, honesty, patience and attentiveness; then it is conceivable that, given time, we might succeed in expanding the territory of our agreement by way of a process of taking stock of what we already hold in common, identifying the crucial points at which we diverge, and then analysing carefully the factors that have brought about that divergence. For disagreement very often turns out to be based on misunderstanding kindled by impatience and carelessness. You state what you think in rough form in order to defend a modest point with which, in itself, I would agree. But, unwittingly, you tread clumsily on something that I hold dear; and I react defensively by launching an attack on what you are defending. Thus we become embroiled in an argument that generates far more heat than light. Sometimes, of course, the disagreement is real and not mistaken, and sometimes its roots go deep and rest on significantly different visions of what it means to flourish as a human being. But even here all is not lost. For, if we are willing to exercise and grow in the relevant virtues, we can exchange questions that test the consistency and the faithfulness to experience of each other's visions, learning why it is that we espouse what we do, exposing weaknesses and oversights and errors, and modifying – and perhaps over time approximating to – the opposing positions.

So, for example, suppose that I think of human well-being primarily in terms of the freedom of the individual and you think of it mainly in terms of the fulfilment of one's role in a community. You might point out to me the extent to which the individual depends upon the community from birth to death, and the obligations that this entails; and I might point out to you the highly conservative implications of your position and ask about the scope it permits for creativity and for social criticism. Eventually, after sustained dialogue, making points, refuting them, defending and conceding them, we might find that out of the clash of theses and antitheses new (and agreed) syntheses have been fashioned.

The point here is not that all moral disagreements will be resolved, certainly not that all moral disagreements can be resolved easily. The point is rather that, if we decline to use disagreement as an excuse for turning away from each other in fear or lazy indifference, and if we are prepared to exercise certain qualities of character, then there is plenty of scope for the effective use of reason in the attempt to build (or augment) a common moral vision. And if there are occasions when a particular attempt is less than successful, there is no need to conclude that it was futile from the beginning. We should not conclude that the disagreement is irresolvable in principle, only that we have not been able to resolve it in fact. Who knows? Perhaps in the next attempt, with more time, greater virtue, and wiser reason, we – or our children – shall succeed.

The lesson that we need to learn from the history of western imperialism, then, is not that we should declare the moralities of foreign cultures immune from criticism. To disengage from others in this way is no mark of genuine respect for them. Instead, we should learn to offer criticism that has first taken the trouble to understand, and is therefore a moment in the course of a dialogue in which we are prepared to play student as much as teacher. We should offer it as one set of human beings to their fellows, and not as the civilized to the savage.

So what is required is a change in the manner and context of our criticism, rather than the wholesale abandonment of it. The truth is, of course, that the latter is not a policy that many of us seriously try to adopt. Regardless of our attitudes to the moral imperialism of the west, few of us hesitate to condemn the custom of female 'circumcision', which is common in many African cultures. And how many of us are prepared to argue against the British suppression in the early-nineteenth century of the Indian custom of *suttee*, according to which widows were expected to immolate themselves on the funeral pyre of their husband; or of the religious cult of *thuggee*, whose devotees served the goddess Kali by the quaint practice of befriending travellers on the road and then, when their trusting backs were turned, strangling them and mutilating their corpses?[7]

Even those of us who are most ardently relativist can be found to hold some moral opinions that we regard as universally valid. It seems, then, that in practice we display more confidence in the possibility of moral knowledge than is strictly allowed us by the theoretical scepticism we tend to confess. We need to ask ourselves what this means. It could mean that we are dishonest or lazy and ought to have the courage or the diligence to align our practice with our theory by ruthlessly expunging all our lingering convictions about moral truth. But such a policy makes no sense, because it would cut the rational ground from under its own feet. It necessarily presupposes certain moral duties: that we ought to be honest and not pretend to know what we have no (sure) grounds for knowing; and that we ought to be consistent. And these in turn presuppose that knowledge of the truth is a value that deserves our most careful handling. A policy of radical moral scepticism, then, necessarily takes for granted what it is committed to eradicate. Not even radical moral sceptics can get by, it seems, without taking at least one value and two moral duties as absolutely certain.

10

But, if these, why not others? Just because we cannot demonstrate with 'scientific' rigour the value of life or friendship, or the obligatory nature of keeping promises and telling the truth, does this mean that such things are so doubtful as to be discounted? As we sure that reality is all of the kind that reveals itself through 'scientific' experiment? Might there not be different dimensions of reality, which are known in different ways? Must knowledge be absolute in order to be regarded as knowledge? Do we have to pretend that what we do not know for certain, we do not know at all? And since human actions and practices – including a policy of radical moral scepticism – can only make sense of themselves ultimately in terms of values that deserve respect, and of duties that are respectful, do we not have reason enough to suppose that we are dealing here with things that are given and not invented, real and not imagined? And does not our reason grow stronger in light of the recognition that these values and duties receive in widely differing human cultures?

It is perfectly true that we ought not to be credulous. We ought not to believe everything that we are told. We ought to doubt when there is good reason to do so. But among the things that we have very good reason to doubt is the reasonableness of an indiscriminate moral scepticism.

So far, in response to the confusion in which moral relativism lands us and the grim implications that it lays out before us, we have reconsidered the proper significance of moral diversity and of post-imperial guilt, as well as our general diffidence in the possibility of moral knowledge. Now we must give second thought to our subjectivist reaction against moral authoritarianism.

It is true that morality often forgets its basic purpose, which is to encourage the kinds of behaviour that help human persons to flourish together. It frequently presents itself as being about obedience to rules, and neglects to consider why the rules are there in the first place. In short, morality inclines toward legalism.

One reason for this, and perhaps the main one, lies in the human desire for control and the fear of losing it. Some of us (at least) find it quite difficult to keep our lives from disintegrating. We experience ourselves as country that is constantly on the verge of breaking out – and breaking down – into civil war. Different desires, all of them legitimate in themselves, clamour for fulfilment; but some cannot be satisfied without frustrating others. Sometimes, for example, the desire for social acceptance wars against that for individual authenticity, or the desire for professional success against domestic flourishing, or the desire for moral integrity against sexual satisfaction. If an individual's life is to have any order and coherence, and if it is not to be paralysed with indecision, then some desires have to be subordinated to others. Subordination need not take the form of sheer repression; it could express itself in terms of the deliberate and reasonable limitation of the scope for satisfaction. Sometimes, however, attachment to one desire is so absolute, and fear of its rivals so intense, that total repression of the latter seems to be the only effective option. In this kind of case, moral rules are often marshalled to provide ideological backing for such a policy; and any attempt by other people to question or qualify the rules is rudely denounced. 'The law must be upheld! There can be no negotiation between Order and Anarchy! Compromise is surrender!'

Legalism, as the insistence upon moral rules but the refusal to reconsider what they are assumed to entail in the light of what they are intended to serve, is the ethical form of a siege-mentality. And as legalists lack the confidence to negotiate with the repressed desire in their own psyches, so they lack the confidence to enter into dialogue with other people who question the law in whose name they repress. Instead, they seek to impose their rigid morality on others, whether by pulling rank, by issuing threats, or by applying force. In their hands, morality becomes a respectable means of oppressive control rather than a guide to the good life.

As a reaction against such legalism, moral subjectivism is to be commended. But it also deserves some commendation in what it affirms as well as in what it denies; and what it affirms is the moral autonomy of the individual.

'Moral autonomy' can mean several things. What it ought to mean is the right of individuals to be allowed to make their own decisions about what they ought to do – the right to be free to follow their own consciences. This is not to claim that whatever an individual decides to do is right. It may well not be. A person's conscience may be mistaken. But it is to claim, nevertheless, that within certain limits that person should not be restrained from following it. There are two reasons for this. The first is that there are situations that are morally grey, where it is not clear what should be done; and in such cases the individual should be allowed to decide according to his or her own best judgement. The other reason is the more basic: namely, that it belongs to human flourishing that human beings order their lives around the service of what is good, and that they do so *voluntarily*. A fulfilled human being is not one who has been programmed or compelled to be good, but one who has freely chosen to be so. As far as is possible, therefore, we should allow other people the freedom to make and execute their own moral choices, even mistaken ones, because unless they are free to choose wrongly they cannot be free to choose rightly. The possibility of virtue, by definition freely chosen, requires the risk of the possibility of freely chosen vice.

Obviously, such moral autonomy cannot be absolute. The freedom to choose must be limited. This is because there are certain kinds of behaviour that a human society cannot tolerate except at its own peril – and which it should not tolerate because they threaten harm to the good of human community. So, for example, someone who is convinced that they ought to 'cleanse' their neighbourhood of sexual immorality by gunning down prostitutes, should not be permitted freedom of conscience.

The kind of moral autonomy that moral subjectivism ought to endorse is the right of an individual to be free, within limits, to make moral choices. But it should not endorse, as it sometimes does, that notion of autonomy which takes it to be equivalent to self-sufficiency. The fact that I am free to make my own mind up does not mean that what I decide is right simply because I decide it. It does not mean that I am free to invent my own morality, or to ignore the moral wisdom that is bequeathed me. It does not mean that I am exempt from having to give adequate reasons for what I do. It does not mean that I am at liberty to withdraw from dialogue with my family and friends, my neighbours and colleagues, and to make a unilateral declaration of moral independence.

Such UDI has its attractions. It promises freedom from constraints, which is widely supposed to be the basic, even the sufficient, condition of human happiness. Whether it is so, and to what extent, is one thing that we shall explore in the chapters that follow.

2

SELF-FULFILMENT
. . . MUST IT BE SELFISH?

Perhaps there have been times and places where the ideal of self-denial or self-sacrifice for the sake of service – whether of God or the neighbour or society or the nation – has been in the ascendant. Perhaps there are cultures where duty is highly regarded, and the emphasis falls heavily on what the individual owes other people. Perhaps this was once true of our own culture, not so long ago.

But self-denial, self-sacrifice and duty are obviously not the dominant norms of our culture today. They speak of an earlier age, which existed certainly before the First World War, and not long after the Second. The norms of our age are different: self-affirmation, self-fulfilment and individual rights. We are suspicious of asceticism: far from being a mark of moral perfection, it seems to us more likely a sign of psychological sickness.

Some people are inclined to regard all this as symptomatic of our moral decline. It seems to them simply degenerate, expressive of unrestrained self-indulgence, selfish and narcissistic. But such a view is mistaken. And it is mistaken for at least three reasons.

One is that the current emphasis on self-affirmation and self-fulfilment is partly a reaction against a culture whose own emphases were often too negative. It should be understood as a corrective counter-emphasis. Friedrich Nietzsche, the mid-nineteenth century German philosopher, is frequently hailed as the prophet of the modern age; and with regard to his celebration of power and beauty and self-realization, this is certainly so. But if Nietzsche represents modernity, then Christianity – or at least a certain version of it – represents the age that ours has supplanted. For Nietzsche's fierce affirmation of life was largely a repudiation of the repressiveness of the pietistic Lutheran Christianity in which he had been brought up. He hated what seemed to him to be Christianity's philistinism, its debilitating moralism and its meanness of spirit. The temper of his point of view is well expressed in the following aphorisms:

> The Christian resolve to find the world ugly and bad has made the world ugly and bad.[1]

> Had he [Jesus] remained in the desert far from the good and the just! Perhaps he would have learned to live and learned to love the earth – and laughter as well![2]

> I should only believe in a God who knows how to dance.[3]

For a dramatic presentation of what the modern affirmation of self-fulfilment is reacting against, watch Ingmar Bergman's semi-autobiographical film, *Fanny and Alexander*.[4] Here, the vibrant colour, the easy vitality, and the sheer fun of the pagan world of the theatre stands in stark contrast to the austere, frigid, resentful, and, in the end, downright cruel world of the Lutheran bishop's household.

One reason, then, why it is a mistake to dismiss as sheer self-indulgence our current devotion to the value of self-fulfilment is that, to some extent, it represents a healthy corrective to the more life-denying culture of our recent past. And it is a corrective that Christians who really believe in the goodness of God and of all that he has made, should find easy to applaud.

Another reason to respect the value of self-fulfilment is to be found in the work of Freud. One of the things that he succeeded in identifying is the psychological mechanism (or, perhaps better, tactic) of repression. This is the procedure whereby we deny strong desires that we do not wish, or feel able, to own. The desire might be for some kind of sexual engagement, for love, or for power. And we might not feel able to own it because we believe that our friends and family will desert us if we do, or that the lives that we have carefully built up for ourselves will fall apart. What Freud identified was that some desires, when summarily dismissed from consciousness, do not simply give up the ghost and cease to exist. Rather, they continue to live, but in the unconscious part of the self instead of the conscious. How do we know this? We know it from the ways in which 'repressed' desires continue to assert themselves outside of full consciousness. One of these ways is in inadvertent behaviour that does not quite make sense in terms of the self's official self-description, and which suggests that more is going on than that description admits. This is what the famous 'Freudian slips' are about – moments when the mask drops to reveal a rather different face. It is also partly what the slightly less famous Jungian 'shadow' is about: the insistent demand (often in dreams) for recognition on the part of a dimension of someone's life that has been too long neglected or denied – typically culminating in the 'mid-life' crisis when, for (dramatic) example, a bank manager with suburban wife and two kids finds himself possessed by an irresistible urge to join a travelling circus and become a trapeze artist.

Part of what the phenomenon of repression tells us is that, in some cases, especially those involving the deep and powerful desires for love and sex, sheer denial is not effective. Indeed, it can often be downright harmful, making the self a permanent battleground and inducing crippling depression. The irrepressible insistence of repressed desires for some kind of recognition requires a different response. It requires something other than uncompromising repudiation. It asks for some kind of negotiation. And this negotiation, as any other, is bound to involve at least a measure of acknowledgement; acknowledgement that something of what is desired is legitimate, and has a right to seek – if not to find – fulfilment.

A third reason why the value of self-fulfilment should be affirmed is that, without it, it is impossible to explain why anyone should do what they believe to be right. 'Why are you doing x?' you ask me. 'Because it's right,' I reply. 'But why bother doing what's right?' you retort. Here, I could answer, 'Because what's right is right.' But that would merely underscore my belief in the value of what's right; it would hardly amount to an explanation of it.

Sooner or later, the explanation for why I or anyone else should bother doing what is right must be given in terms of self-fulfilment. The ultimate reason why we should bother doing what is right is that, one way or another, it is good for us. It benefits us. It helps to fulfil us. For what reason could I possibly have for doing something that benefits me in no way at all, not now or later, neither materially nor spiritually? What reason could I possibly have for doing something that *simply* harms or destroys me? Even the masochist seeks pleasure through his pain. Self-fulfilment, or the promotion of one's own good, is the ultimate rationale for any human act.

But surely to say this is to make all human action, including action that claims to be 'moral', essentially selfish? No, it does not. It does make it essentially self-interested; but self-interestedness is not necessarily the same thing as selfishness. 'Selfishness' refers to behaviour that seeks to serve the self only or without due regard for other people. Selfishness is self-centred, ego-centric. Self-interestedness, however, need not be.

I might suppose that it is in my own self-interest to behave selfishly. I might think that I'm doing myself a favour in being selfish. If I did, then my understanding of what is in my interest, of my own good, would make it reasonable for me to go around grabbing as much of what I want as I can, and fending off all other claims. It would make it reasonable for me to use and manipulate other people in order to satisfy my physical and emotional needs. It would make it reasonable for me to use the piled corpses of betrayed friendships as steps on which to mount to the top of whatever social or professional pyramid I am climbing.

However, there are at least two reasons for challenging this selfish reading of self-interest. The first is that it is inefficient, even counter-productive. People who behave selfishly, manipulatively, or ruthlessly, alienate themselves from other people. At the very least they are not trusted. At best, others will lend their co-operation only with reluctance, and then only with caution. At worst, they will withdraw co-operation altogether and engage in passive or active hostility. Utter selfishness engenders resentment and opposition. It gets in its own way. Paradoxically, then, there is a selfish reason for paying some attention to the just claims of others. There is a selfish reason for moderating one's own selfishness.

But there is also a very different kind of reason. And this is that human beings are not designed to be selfish. What is being claimed here is that human beings flourish when they pay active attention to the needs and rights of others. The most fulfilled human beings, the most fully human, are not those who grab but those who give, not the Robert Maxwells of this world but the Mother Teresas. It belongs to *human* self-interest precisely to give oneself in the service of others, precisely not to be selfish.

'Well,' someone might say, 'that sounds all very nice and noble, but is it really true? Are not selfish, manipulative, ruthless people often very successful and perfectly happy? How can it be said that they do not flourish? And are not those who devote themselves to the service of others often abused and exploited? How can it be said that they flourish?'

It is certainly true that people who behave selfishly can, in spite of the damage they do and the resentment and opposition they provoke, be very successful in getting what they want. And they may also be very happy in enjoying what they get. In one of Woody Allen's finest films, *Crimes and Misdemeanors*,[5] Judah, a wealthy and distinguished New York eye-specialist, adored by his family and lauded by his community, hires a professional assassin to dispose of his mistress before she tells his wife of their affair and brings everything that he has so carefully built – his marriage, his reputation, his status – tumbling down about his ears. Immediately after the murder, Judah is wracked by guilt and almost brings himself to find relief by confessing his crime. But, as time passes, his conscience becomes dull and in the end he seems to succeed entirely in erasing the memory of what he has done, and in carrying on with his life perfectly intact. Sometimes, perhaps all too often, the wicked not only get away with their wicked deeds, but they actually seem to prosper as a result of them. How, then, can it be said that those who pursue their own interests selfishly and ruthlessly are not fulfilled?

One possible response is to say that appearances deceive. It is to claim that the person who has spent his life feeding himself at the expense of others is bound always to be haunted by the sense of being isolated and vulnerable, by the fear of betrayal and attack, by paranoia. That may well be. Certainly, the appearance of equilibrium or contentedness should not be taken at face value. A moment's honest self-reflection should be enough to persuade anyone of the yawning discrepancy between the public self that is filtered to the world out there, and the private self that lurks just behind the eyes. Those who seem content are not necessarily so; that is why news of a suicide so often comes as a complete shock. 'Why did he do it?' friends ask themselves in bewilderment. 'He was such good fun. There was always a smile on his face. He seemed so together.'

Seemed.

But beyond reason to doubt how genuine is the happiness of the selfish person, there is also reason to doubt their well-being. Where 'happiness' refers to someone's state of mind, 'well-being' refers to something more objective – to someone's character, for example, or to their relationships. If we can raise reasonable, if inconclusive, doubts about the genuineness of a selfish person's happiness, we can raise more certain doubts about the well-being of their character and relationships.

Woody Allen's Judah may have succeeded in banishing from his mind disturbing memories of what he had done, but he certainly has not succeeded in banishing *from himself* the effects of his deed. He may no longer be kept awake at night by the thought of being a murderer, but a murderer he still is. More than that, he is a murderer who has learned to live with what he has done. And he has learned to live with it, not by owning his crime and then repudiating himself as criminal, not by repenting; but rather by pretending that he never did it, or that it is of little account if he did. And because he is a murderer who has learned to come to terms with himself in this way, he has made himself into the kind of person who is internally capable of doing anything. For he has dismantled all the internal, psychological, subjective constraints upon doing horrendous acts. He has found a way of committing murder without allowing his crime to disturb his slumbers.

What applies to murderers applies also to people who are merely selfish. They may not be disturbed by their selfishness, their happiness may be intact. But they *are* (at least in some respects) selfish; and their being selfish, their having a selfish character, determines the range of things that they are strongly inclined to do, and the range of things that they are virtually incapable of doing. Who someone is, determines the shape of that person's actual freedom to act. People who are selfish will have a limited ability to see beyond their own wants and feelings to recognize the needs and rights of others. So, for example, such a person, driven by his own fierce libidinal want to possess someone who will love him, will be utterly oblivious to his beloved's need for a certain distance, a certain space to breathe, a certain freedom to be herself and not just someone else's lover. A selfish person is more or less handicapped in his ability to *see* what is not himself.

Selfish people might *feel* happy, but selfish they nevertheless *are*; and because of who they are, they are capable of relating to other people only in selfish kinds of ways. As a consequence, some levels and qualities of relationship will be beyond them completely. Others will not trust them and will not give them the gift of their unguarded selves. And their attempts to build and maintain any relationship will always be hindered and threatened by a selfishness that gives too little and demands too much.

It could be argued that selfish people might be happy enough with such a level and quality of relationship as they have got, since they do not know what they are missing. Can we say, then, that they do not flourish? Surely, we can. Even if it were simply true that alcoholics are happy so long as they are drunk, heroin addicts so long as they are high, masochists so long as they are being hurt and sadists so long as they are hurting; even if all this were true, we could still reasonably say that none of them were flourishing. We could still doubt their well-being. We could doubt it with reason in so far as the phenomenon of a happy fool is immediately recognizable to us: the phenomenon of someone who is content to live his life at a very immature or even subhuman level, without having taken the trouble to explore all the other possibilities. We could also reasonably doubt their well-being because of their lack of freedom; because of their being driven by physical and psychological passions; because of their inability to pay attention to anything other than the next drink or the next fix; because their addiction is leading them to kill themselves. There is a lot more to human well-being, to human fulfilment, than pleasurable states of mind. The kinds of human being that we instinctively admire, whom we recognize to have matured somewhat in humanity, are generally not those who sit slumped in some happy, drug-induced trance, but rather those who have engaged successfully with life, those who have invested themselves in building something worthwhile. We admire those who have actively moved out into the world, not those who lie passively turned in upon themselves.

Selfish people may be happy, but they do not flourish. But what about selfless people who, in or because of their service to others, are abused or exploited or injured? How can they be said to flourish in their suffering?

We are familiar enough with the phenomenon of adults who devote themselves to taking care of a parent, and who consequently never seem to develop lives of their own. It is as if they exist entirely to meet the parent's wants. Often it seems that there is something distinctly unhealthy about such a situation. It seems that the parent's demands are unwarranted and unfair; and that their son or daughter's acquiescence has a pathological quality about it. Their service seems akin to a form of voluntary slavery.

The point to note here is that selflessness is not all of a piece. There are some ways of being unselfish in which we do not flourish. This is so when one's selflessness is less an expression of love for another than it is of contempt for the self. And as such it is wrong. It is wrong because there are duties that we owe ourselves as well as duties we owe other people. We too have a value that deserves respect – even our own. We are required to love our neighbour as, and not instead of, ourselves. This means that we have a duty to resist unjust claims upon us. The fact that Mummy would be terribly lonely and feel cruelly abandoned if little Philip (aged forty-two) ever left home, and the fact that Philip should be grateful to Mummy for all that she has done for him (as she reminds him daily), does not mean that she has a right to forbid him to see another woman – or to insist that, if he were to marry, she should be allowed to move in with the newly weds. One person's want does not amount to another person's duty; and being strong in love precisely does *not* involve giving whatever is demanded.

Nevertheless, it remains true that caring for other people, even when one's own motivation is healthy and one's action is an expression of genuine love, can be costly. Sometimes, respect for another's freedom or for another's trust requires the painful foregoing of one's own wants. And if we would be reconciled to someone who has hurt us, then we need to forgive; and since injury can never be undone (even by compensation), forgiveness always requires of the forgiver that they simply absorb it, bear it, suffer it. But, if that is true, then how can it be claimed that love is that state of being for which humans are made, and in which they flourish and are fulfilled? For how can self-fulfilment be compatible with suffering?

As has been argued already, human self-fulfilment is not equivalent to a pleasurable state of consciousness. It is more active and objective than that. It refers more to a state of being engaged than to a state of mere physical or mental sensation. It is possible to *be* well, then, without *feeling* good. But that does not quite capture the matter; for there are different levels of feeling. At one level I might be painfully aware of the loss of time to myself, or of disposable income, or of sleep that my care of an aged parent or a young child is costing me. The thought of it might make me groan aloud. But at the same time, on another level, I can experience the deep pleasure – or, perhaps better, the deep satisfaction – of knowing that I am doing right, of knowing that I am investing myself in something intrinsically worthwhile. In the midst of more or less severe suffering, I can have a strong sense of my being well invested, and therefore of my own value and integrity. And this sense, this knowledge is actually worth the pain. In spite of suffering, I am aware of being fulfilled.

Something like this is poignantly affirmed in Jeannette Winterson's novel, *Written on the Body*, where the main character reflects on her grief at the sudden death of someone she had loved:

'You'll get over it . . .' It's the clichés that cause the trouble. To lose someone you love is to alter your life for ever. You don't get over it because 'It' is the person you loved. The pain stops, there are new people, but the gap never closes. How could it? The particularness of someone who mattered enough to grieve over is not made anodyne by death. This hole in my heart is in the shape of you and no-one else can fit it. Why would I want them to?

I've thought a lot about death recently, the finality of it, the argument ending in mid-air. One of us hadn't finished, why did the other one go? And why without warning?

. . . The day before the Wednesday last, this time a year ago, you were here and now you're not. Why not? Death reduces us to the baffled logic of a small child. If yesterday why not today? And where are you?

Fragile creatures of a small blue planet, surrounded by light-years of silent space. Do the dead find peace beyond the rattle of the world? What peace is there for us whose best love cannot return to them even for a day? I raise my head to the door and think I will see you in the frame. I know it is your voice in the corridor but when I run outside the corridor is empty. There is nothing I can do that will make any difference. The last word was yours.

The fluttering in the stomach goes away and the dull waking pain. Sometimes I think of you and feel giddy. Memory makes me lightheaded, drunk on champagne. All the things we did. And if anyone had said this was the price, I would have agreed to pay it. That surprises me; that with the hurt and the mess comes a shaft of recognition. It was worth it. Love is worth it.[6]

The presence of pain need not signal the absence of self-fulfilment.

But what about death? In what sense could someone who dies in the service of other people be described as 'fulfilled'? How can self-fulfilment be compatible with the very loss of one's own life?

But there is a prior question to ask. It generally makes sense, before enquiring about *how* something *could* be, to ask first *whether* in fact it *is*. For it may well be possible to establish its existence before being able to explain it.

So, first, is self-fulfilment compatible with losing one's life in the service of others? According to the testimony given on the eve of their death by some of those who have lost their lives in this way, and according to the testimony of those who have beheld the self-sacrifice of such people, the answer would seem to be, Yes. In so far as we admire martyrs who give their lives in some noble cause, in so far as we regard their acts as heroic rather than foolish, we assume that in their martyrdom these people have achieved a certain profound fulfilment of their humanity. We do not admire them on account of their effectiveness, because those who give their lives in the cause of, say, justice have not necessarily been successful in defending it. Indeed, the very fact that they have come to the point of having to give up their lives may well be precisely because their defence has failed. We do not admire martyrs because of their success, but because of their beauty; because in their acts of self-sacrifice they shine with the goodness in which they have invested themselves entirely. We admire them as shining examples of the fullness of humanity.

Our own instinctive assumption as third-party spectators is corroborated by the subjective experience of at least some of those who have looked upon their own impending martyrdom.

Take the example of Helmuth James von Moltke. Born in 1907 the son of an English mother, he was a member of the Prussian aristocracy and was the great-nephew of Bismarck's greatest general. He was a lawyer by profession and was embarked on a high-flying career when the National Socialist Party came to power in Germany under Hitler. A man of deep Christian conviction and humanitarian commitment, von Moltke set himself to oppose Nazism – and in 1934 we could have found him in All Souls College, Oxford, earnestly engaged in trying to persuade some Fellows there that the Third Reich could not be tamed by a policy of appeasement. When the Second World War came he joined the Abwehr, the German Intelligence Service, as a legal advisor on international law. In that post he strove to do what he could to resist and ameliorate the increasingly ruthless policies of the Nazi regime toward prisoners-of-war and Jews. He also began to gather around himself an ecumenical group of like-minded men – later known as the Kreisau Circle – to discuss and plan for the reconstruction of Germany after Hitler. In January 1944 von Moltke was arrested, and subsequently fell under (false) suspicion of being implicated in the von Stauffenberg plot to assassinate Hitler. Just over a year later he was tried, condemned to death and executed.

It would have been quite understandable if he had gone to his death in sheer despair. For his strenuous work in resisting the Nazi regime had done very little, if anything, to bring it down. And what it certainly had done was to abort all the dreams and plans he had had for his career and his family, and to bring him to the gallows at the age of thirty-eight. It might well have seemed to him that all his work had come to naught – and worse.

But that's not how he saw it. On the day he was condemned to death he wrote a letter to his wife that was almost euphoric. In it he spoke of what had befallen him as the climax, not the nadir, of his life. It felt to him that everything had been leading to this point; that all his life's work was about to find its fulfilment, its final integrity, in the moment of his death. Echoing and paraphrasing the last words of Jesus on the cross, he wrote: 'My life is finished and I can say of myself: He died in the fullness of years and of life's experience . . . The task for which God has made me is done.'[7]

There is evidence in the experience of martyrdom, both on the part of those undergoing it and on the part of those admiring it, that self-fulfilment and suffering to the point of losing one's life are, in fact, compatible. But how can that be so? Surely someone who loses their life has lost *everything*. How, then, could they be said to fulfil themselves?

How, indeed?

There are two possible ways out of this quandary. One is to question our admiration for martyrs and to wonder whether, in fact, we should not rather pity those who squander everything for the sake of making a futile gesture. We could consider regarding martyrs as idealistic fools. The price of this, however, would be a grim deflation in our estimation of human beings. Instead of being such as complete themselves in devotion to what is true and good, humans would henceforth appear to us small, grubby and egotistical beings, for whom reasonable behaviour is reduced, in the end, to saving one's own skin at all costs. Certainly, such a grim estimate of human beings might conceivably be the truth. But we should hardly welcome it with open arms; and if there is an alternative way of reconciling self-fulfilment and death, we should prefer it. So, instead of doubting our instinctive admiration for martyrs, we should rather question our assumption that to die is to lose everything.

It is commonly assumed that in the contemporary west religious beliefs, such as belief in life after death, are on the wane. It is frequently taken for granted that 'modern' people cannot believe such things. There is, however, some good reason to doubt such assumptions. They are usually made by people educated in the 1950s and 1960s when it did seem as if religion was receding before the relentless tide of secularism. Nowadays that picture of events appears substantially mistaken. For whereas it is true (in Western Europe) that traditional Christian belief and practice have been losing their appeal, and that church attendance has been declining, it is not true that 'modern' people in a supposedly secularized society such as Britain have been becoming simply non-religious. Indeed, one piece of social scientific research has found that about 70 per cent of British adults claim to have had a significant 'religious' experience.[8] People may find themselves alienated from much institutional religion; but that does not mean that they repudiate religious experience or even religious belief and practice that is less formal and dogmatic, more private and immediate.

There are, then, plenty of 'modern' people who, despite not going to church, nevertheless hold religious beliefs of one sort or another; and among these will often be the belief in life after death. Those who hold such a belief at all firmly might well also hold what it implies: that to die is not necessarily to lose everything. But for those who are not so sure that there is an after-life, and for those who assume that there is not, here are two reasons in favour of its existence.

The first is that some of our deeply rooted moral convictions require it in order to make sense. We are strongly inclined to regard those who give their lives for some noble cause as heroic rather than foolish. But such a view would not make sense if, in dying, such people lost absolutely everything. In order to be intelligible our high esteem of martyrs requires belief in life after death. Immanuel Kant argued roughly along these lines when he described immortality as a 'postulate' (that is, a fundamental assumption) of 'practical' or 'moral' reason.[9]

This basic assumption of one of our deeply held moral convictions is corroborated by the event which the original Christians attested and upon which the specifically Christian view of the world is founded: the resurrection of Jesus of Nazareth from the dead. Jesus was put to death in large measure because of his conviction that the way of compassion and forgiveness is the way of God, and because of his consequent criticism of the oppressiveness of much current institutional religion. He chose to let himself be killed rather than abandon the cause of humane justice. After his execution by crucifixion his followers were understandably disillusioned. It must have seemed to them that all the hopes that he had inspired had come to nought. Maybe in the bitterness of disappointment some of them even began to think of him as a naive fool. They would not have been the first.

Then came reports that the tomb where his body had been buried had been found empty – though since these were brought by women, no one was very inclined to take them seriously: 'these words seemed to them an idle tale, and they did not believe them'.[10]

But then Jesus himself appeared. In strange form, but recognizable. Not once but several times. And to different groups of people.

Or so it is claimed.

Whether this claim is true or not is beyond proof either way. But there are reasons that tell in its favour: for example, if it were not true, then the bursting of the Christian movement into vigorous life out of the ashes of the crucifixion is hard to explain convincingly.[11] And the belief in the after-life implied by our instinctive esteem for martyrs should at least clear the ground of materialist prejudice, make the notion of a resurrection from the dead initially plausible, and incline us to consider the Christian claim sympathetically.

As with the Resurrection, so with the after-life: belief in it may not be able to command proof, but it can call upon good reasons. It is reasonable as well as humane, then, to suppose that those who suffer death in the cause of upholding the truth or defending justice have nevertheless gained rather than lost themselves. For if there is an after-life, then the notion of pursuing self-fulfilment unselfishly, even to the point of suffering death, makes good sense.

3

FREEDOM
. . . FOR WHAT?

'Freedom' is the modern pass-word. Anyone who wants to be numbered in the ranks of right-thinking people, anyone who does not want to be dismissed out of hand as 'medieval' or reactionary, must confess it in the opening article of their creed. Of all those things that we assume to be essential ingredients of self-fulfilment, freedom surely comes top of the list.

But quite what it is that we are affirming when we say, 'I believe in freedom', is not self-evident, for 'freedom' can mean all sorts of things. It can take a variety of forms: political, economic, sexual, artistic, intellectual and spiritual, for example. There are as many different kinds of freedom as there are spheres of human activity. But to know what any kind of freedom actually involves we need to press two questions in particular: Freedom *from* what? And freedom *for* what? The answers to these questions will help to give us some definite notion of what is being talked about.

So, in espousing freedom as a value, what is it that we value freedom from?

One thing we want freedom from is authority. In our own culture in times past and in other cultures today 'authority' does not carry such negative connotations as it does among us now. Other peoples are more or less happy to defer to the presumed wisdom of those 'in authority'. They trust them to know the truth and to make the right decisions. We, on the whole, do not trust them and do not defer.

'On the whole': for there are exceptions. In modern times, for example, we have tended to defer to the authority of natural

30

scientists. To them we have looked for truth that is really objective and does useful things like save us from drought, from infertility, from cancer, from environmental catastrophe, and from AIDS. Until recently, they have functioned among us as largely unquestioned authorities. But there are signs that even here our faith has begun to weaken. For example, the moral authority of scientists has suffered in the wake of the development of globally devastating weaponry out of the fruits of nuclear science, and also in the wake of the macabre possibilities opened up by medical science. Moreover, the pretensions of natural scientists to possess exclusive access to truly objective knowledge have been severely deflated by assaults on two fronts: by sociological studies that have exposed the role that social and political forces play in shaping the scientific orthodoxy of the day; and by philosophical studies that have alerted us to the more subjective and interpretative dimensions of scientific knowledge.

Still, even if our deference to the authority of those with a claim to expertise in grasping and taming the natural world is not quite what it was, it is still far greater than any we pay to those with some traditional claim to expert knowledge of religious or moral reality – whether they be priest or teacher or parent. With regard to questions about the ultimate context of human life, or about what we should value and what we should or should not do, we tend not simply to accept what we are told by other people. We do not defer to the pronouncements of religious or moral authorities.

Why not? Why do we not accept what we are told about religious reality or moral life in the same way that we tend to accept what we are told about material reality?

One reason is that the truths of natural science are often very far removed from the truths of common sense. Our eyes tell us that the earth stands still while the sun moves across the horizon. Science tells us that it is we who are moving and not the sun. Our touch assures us that the table before us is solid and stable. Science tells us that the elementary constituents of our table are in constant motion. In many instances the truths of science are a long way from the truths of common sense, and an abstract and sophisticated intelligence is required to get from one to the other. So we defer to the authority of those with the necessary training and expertise.

Regarding religious and moral reality, in contrast, we tend to assume that we have direct access. We do not need to rely on what others say, because we can check it out for ourselves against our own experience. The priest says: 'God exists.' We say: 'I haven't seen him.' Mother says: 'You shouldn't sleep around.' We say: 'So long as it's safe and by mutual consent and nobody gets hurt, what's the problem?'

Another reason why we do not readily accept religious or moral authority is that we are inclined to associate it with authoritarianism. We associate religious authority with the experience of being told what to believe about God and of having our doubts and questions silenced by appeals to mystery or threats of hell-fire. And we associate moral authority with the experience of having a series of moral rules imposed on us by someone who has not taken the care to pay serious attention to the awkward details presented by our personalities and our predicaments. With good reason we do not trust religious or moral assertions that simply do not square with our experience; and we do not trust religious or moral authorities who do not take the trouble to try to make them square.

Now, it is not the case, of course, that all instances of religious or moral authority are authoritarian. There are plenty of examples of priests and teachers and parents who listen before they speak, who take critical questions seriously and handle them with care, who argue rather than pontificate. Why, then, do these formal authorities still connote authoritarianism?

For some people, no doubt, it is because they have suffered direct experience of it. For others, it is because their parents have suffered it and because they have not yet discovered that their parents' experience is not universal. But for many people who have neither direct nor indirect experience upon which to ground it, the connotation is something that they accept on the authority of a prevailing cultural ethos sustained in part by media that tend to regard iconoclastic assaults on 'establishment' religion as intrinsically more attention-worthy than defences of it. That is one of the reasons why, when people think of Christianity, they often think first of the Crusades, the

Inquisition, opposition to Galileo and Darwin, and religious strife in Northern Ireland, rather than, for example, the founding of hospitals and schools in the Middle Ages, the movements for the reform of prisons and the abolition of slavery in the eighteenth and nineteenth centuries, and the influence of Archbishop William Temple in bringing about the creation of the Welfare State during and after the Second World War.

Still, even if we sometimes expect authority to be authoritarian when it is not, we are certainly right to want to be free from it when it is. It belongs to human dignity that we have the responsibility to reason, and to reason honestly; and we offend against our dignity when we assent to what we are told simply because it might cost us if we do not.

In addition to freedom from authority, we also want freedom from custom or tradition. We do not want to be bound by the past, by its patterns of thought or behaviour. We do not want just to follow in the footsteps of our parents. Nowadays we tend to assume that what is old is tired and obsolete. This attitude is interesting. It is interesting because there are and have been cultures where the opposite is assumed; where the past is considered home to the Golden Age, and the point of the present is to make the future as much like the past as possible. Which way a culture turns depends, presumably, on how disturbed the present is, what the prospects are for settling it in an innovative and imaginative way, and how courageous the culture feels about trying something new. If the prospects are not good and the culture lacks confidence, it will tend to idealize the past and try to take refuge in it. But if the prospects are fair and the mood confident, it will turn the other way.

Modern western culture in general has been propelled by the conviction that history is a forward movement of inexorable progress – a quasi-religious conviction that is a secularized version of the Judaeo-Christian belief that God is in the process of establishing his kingdom on earth. So western culture is fundamentally future-oriented and optimistic; and what is true of the modern west is also true of Britain, most markedly so in the late-Victorian period and the decades immediately following the Second World War.

In itself, the hope and expectation that the future will be

better than the present need not be tied to a general disposition to denigrate the past. It is quite consistent to want change and to work for it while happily acknowledging one's debts to the past. Such debts are inevitable, for no plans for the future, no matter how innovative, are invented entirely from scratch.

So why have we been disposed to regard the past as something to be left behind? Why have we presumed that what is 'modern' is an improvement upon what is not? Why have we taken up a general prejudice against what is old?

Part of the answer to this is simply that the old has sometimes been challenged and (at least apparently) found wanting. In Britain, for example, traditional habits of deference to social authorities were severely shaken by the costly incompetence of the military leadership during the First World War. And throughout the west, traditional sexual mores seem to have lost much of their sense in an age when effective contraceptives are readily available.

However, a larger part of the answer has to do with the emergence of youth culture and, more precisely, of a cult of youth. The growth of a distinct youth culture, fostered by commercial interests eager to exploit the unprecedented affluence of young people since the 1950s, has in itself encouraged a sense of mutual alienation between children and their parents. But more decisive in creating a general prejudice against the old has been the propagation of the *normativity* of the perspective of the adolescent. The success of this has been such that the attitudes of young people who fashion themselves after the likes of James Dean have become the assumptions of the culture as a whole.

It is not that the perspective of the adolescent has nothing worthwhile to offer. It does. It has the virtue of questioning received wisdom, and of challenging the tired resignation of the middle-aged with an energetic idealism. Adolescents are often alert enough to see things that their elders have long grown accustomed to overlooking. But adolescents, too, have their blindspots. Typically committed to forging a distinctive identity for themselves, they are heavily predisposed not to acknowledge the extent to which they depend upon their parents and upon wider society. In order to take control of their present and make it their own, they have to repudiate the past. Or, at least, they have to repudiate facets of it; for only a very few adolescents actually go as far as to leave home and opt out altogether. So one thing that an adolescent perspective obscures is the extent to which, even in the throes of rebellion, we continue to depend on what has been given us. Such a perspective does not encourage a *discriminate* coming to terms with the past, distinguishing what should be retained from what should be discarded. Instead of regarding tradition as something that, with careful and critical scrutiny, might yield a wealth of resources for coping with the present and building the future, it sees it only as a prison from which to escape.

There are signs, however, that the cultural dominance of the adolescent's perspective is beginning to weaken. Nowadays, the word 'modern' has begun to seem distinctly shopworn. It belongs, above all, to the 1950s and 60s, years, not just of rejuvenation, but also of cocky impatience with a tired and stuffy status quo, and of much blind enthusiasm for sheer novelty. Now, thirty years on, so many of the aspirations of that era seem naive, so much of its energy mere effervescence. Before the end of the 1980s many of the brash 'modern' buildings erected twenty years earlier were, symbolically, already crumbling. Whereas in the 1960s whatever was bright and fast and novel was hailed as 'modern' and had claim, thereby, to be riding the tide of history, now much of it just seems washed up.

In the 1990s we are beginning to think of ourselves as 'postmodern'. Part of what we mean by this is that we have a more mature awareness of the limits that prevent us from transcending the past altogether; of the way in which rebellion invariably bears the marks of the status quo, and revolution so often ends up reproducing a different form of the same Old Regime. We post-moderns are more sober about the possibilities of change.

We are also less inclined to see ourselves as having to choose between polar opposites – for example, between Tradition or Modernity. We are more eclectic. And although eclecticism can, and often does, degenerate into a kind of shallow, supermarket, dilettantism, it can also be expressive of a more discriminating judgement. So even if we are extremely cagey about committing ourselves to a particular tradition, we are more willing than our counterparts in the 1960s to recognize the value of the traditional, and to be willing to avail ourselves of its riches. In so far as advertising has its finger on the pulse of the contemporary mood – and if it does not, then it will not succeed in selling anything – it is notable how much appeal has been made in recent years, not to the glamour of the Future but to the simplicity and dependability of the Past. Some may dismiss this as symptomatic of the yearning for the securities of a mythical, bygone age on the part of those who face an uncertain future. No doubt, to some extent it is. But it may also be as indicative of wisdom as it is of nostalgia. It may express awareness that there is much of value that the past has to offer the present, and that we are not the first human beings to have lived and learned and built something worthwhile.

Authority and tradition: those are two of the things from which we tend, or have tended until recently, to want freedom. A third is dependence.

It is natural for human beings to want a measure of independence from other people. It is of great importance to our well-being that we have space for the exercise of responsibility and a certain scope for self-determination. To have such space and scope is a vital part of what being an adult human being is. Adolescents locked in combat with their parents know it. Women in protest against male chauvinism know it. Employees out on strike against their employers know it. Nationalists in rebellion against their colonial masters know it. For often it is precisely room for responsibility and self-determination that such people are struggling for. They know just how oppressive and humiliating excessive dependence on others can be.

This is also sometimes the experience of people who have fallen in love. They find themselves obsessed with their beloved. Unable to think of anyone or anything else. Unable to value themselves apart from the one they love. Desperate for her (or his) affirmation and attention. Feeling entirely empty inside without it, worthless, lifeless. Their emotional dependence is absolute. At the time, it seems that such love is life itself, despite the pain it entails. But afterward, when the passion has subsided – whether because love was never requited, or because it was – the lover shudders at the very thought of his emotional dependence. At the childish intensity of it. At its lack of dignity. And maybe, too, at the unfairness of it to the one he loved, whom he had unilaterally burdened with the task of endowing his life with meaning.

There are good reasons, therefore, for wanting to avoid excessive dependence on other people. Equally, however, there are reasons to avoid excessive independence. Neither excess is appropriate for adults: the first characterizes the child; the second, the adolescent. Mature human beings are certainly those who can distinguish themselves from other people; who will take responsibility for themselves and respect the freedom of others to give or withhold themselves; who will live their own lives and let others be free to live theirs. But mature human beings are not people who pretend to self-sufficiency. They are not those who think that they do not need others. On the contrary, they are quite aware of the limitations of their own abilities. They are mindful that so much that they now possess was given them, or at least depends upon what was given them. And they also know that they cannot enter into love without being open to receive. So, while observing the bounds of respect, they are prepared to ask for help. They are prepared to dignify others by allowing them to give something valuable.

Depending on others is, of course, a risky business. It makes us vulnerable to disappointment, sometimes bitter and severe. But the alternative has its own risks, too. These are the risks of isolation: of cracking up under the strain because you could not bring yourself to admit your weakness and ask for help; of losing touch with reality because you would not allow your own vision of things to be tested against other people's; and of hurting those who would care for you by (at least implicitly) demeaning the value of what they would give you. So the choice is not between one way that is risky and one that is safe. It is between a way that is honest and open and generous, and one that is fearful and brittle and, in the end, mean. The mature human being will prefer the risk of disappointment to the risk of isolation.

Closely allied to our fear of dependence is our fear of commitment. Both are born, to some extent, of mistrust. In the first case we fear being let down. In the second we fear being eaten up. Experience may have given us good reason to fear so. As children we may have found ourselves called upon by an unhappy parent to meet some seemingly vast emotional need – to substitute, for example, for an alienated spouse. Or as adolescents or adults we may have found ourselves involved in an intimate relationship in which we felt trapped, obstructed on the one hand by demands we did not want to meet, but, on the other, by a guilt that would not let us run away. In both cases, and in many others like them, the needs or demands of another person have threatened to overwhelm and consume us. Naturally, it has made us shy of committing ourselves at all, and very shy indeed of committing ourselves without explicit reservation. Keeping the back door open has acquired an urgent importance for us.

In so far as our maintaining a measure of freedom from commitment is provisional, it makes good sense. It would be foolish, even disastrous, to commit ourselves to someone at all seriously without first being sure that they respect us. And for someone to respect us means that they distinguish between themselves and us, that they recognize that we are an *other*. It means that they acknowledge that their destiny and ours are not the same, and that it is no more our job to give their lives meaning and purpose than it is theirs to do the same for us. It makes sense to hold back from commitment until we are assured – as assured as one reasonably can be – that, should we commit ourselves, we will not find our very identities under threat. For only with such assurance could we ever be free to volunteer ourselves into another's hands.

Nevertheless, reserving oneself can become a bad and stifling habit. Instead of being a tactic, it becomes a principle. We withhold ourselves from commitment here and now because it is always possible that there might be a better deal around the corner. And besides, we like travelling. We like the novelty and variety and risk of exploring foreign parts. We do not want to get tied down by obligations. We want to be free to pack up our tent and take off at will.

The freedom to explore is certainly an important ingredient of what makes human life worth living. But when it becomes the only kind of freedom that we recognize, then it threatens to become a kind of prison. For if freedom for breadth is the only freedom we value and cultivate, then our freedom for depth will wither. If we would be free to go deep, then we must be willing to suffer restriction upon our surface-movements.

This is not just a matter of the allocation of limited time and energies. It is also a matter of the choosing and building of the self, the development of a particular character, the fostering of some skills and strengths at the expense of others. For the habits and skills of the globe-trotter are not – and never could be – the habits and skills necessary for building a home and a community. And only the habits and skills of the sexual nomad can be cultivated instead of those needed to plumb the depths of one particular relationship.

We speak here of the choice between breadth and depth. Equally, with Milan Kundera, we could speak of the choice between lightness and heaviness:

> But is heaviness truly deplorable and lightness splendid? The heaviest of burdens crushes us, we sink beneath it, it pins us to the ground. But in the love poetry of every age, the woman longs to be weighed down by the man's body. The heaviest of burdens is therefore simultaneously an image of life's most intense fulfilment. The heavier the burden, the closer our lives come to the earth, the more real and truthful they become. Conversely, the absolute absence of a burden causes man to be lighter than air, to soar into the heights, take leave of the earth and his earthly being, and become only half real, his movements as free as they are insignificant. What then shall we choose? Weight or lightness?[1]

The illustration is sexist, but the point it depicts is valid: to be free from commitments, from the restrictions that obligations to others place upon us, is actually to be bereft of a vital means of human fulfilment. And the more we are in the habit of such freedom, the more unable we become to exchange it for something else. We lose the freedom to choose commitment. We become trapped on the surface, condemned always to wander, never to come home. There comes a time when the habitual dilettante simply cannot turn into a connoisseur. Thus, freedom can grow into a kind of slavery that stunts the growth of our humanity, and robs us of the ultimate satisfaction of being able to love deeply.

Moreover, to be bereft of ties and obligations is to be bereft to a large extent of a sense of one's own worth. In a situation where no one depends on you, no one expects anything from you, what you do ceases to have much value. When we first leave home and go to university, for example, our freedom from the demands of being a member of a family and a school can be quite exhilarating. We are almost entirely free to choose to whom we relate and how we run our lives. We have the liberty to roam and explore and experiment. And that can be exciting. But at the same time we can also be half-aware of an underlying mood of indefinite insecurity. Not only because of the pressures of academic and social competition, but also because we find ourselves in a kind of limbo. Uprooted. Unconnected. Free-floating.

Being on holiday can sometimes give rise to a similar experience, especially if our time is largely unstructured. Initially, we feel relief. We are far enough away from the demands of our work to be able to relax. We get up late. We go for walks. We see the sights. We doze in the afternoon (if we're middle-aged or thereabouts). We even allow ourselves to get engrossed in a fat novel. But, then, after a week or two we begin to get restless. Sight-seeing starts to bore. We run out of books to read. We begin to day-dream about our work. We find ourselves making plans for when we get back to the office. Then it dawns on us that we actually want to go home and get stuck into real life again.

Human nature abhors too much of a vacuum. It is important for us to have a place, a role, a function that other people recognize and value. Otherwise, we find it difficult to feel that we are valuable. That is why people who are unemployed for a long time tend to get depressed. Freedom from social ties and commitments is fine for a change. But when it becomes normal it degenerates into a mood of isolation, of purposelessness and meaninglessness.

So far, we have considered some of the things *from* which we tend to want freedom: authority, tradition, dependence and commitment. Now it is time to take a look at the other, positive side of the coin: at what it is that we want freedom *for*.

One object of our freedom is choice. The fact that 'freedom of choice' has been a (perhaps *the*) principle behind much of the policy of recent Conservative governments in Britain is not sufficient to warrant its immediate dismissal by those of contrary political persuasion. For such freedom is an important element of human well-being. Human beings flourish when they have scope for taking responsibility, for making decisions, for choosing between available options. It belongs to our specific dignity. Without such freedom, we feel out of control, oppressed, frustrated, angry.

But not all choices, of course, are of the same order. There is the choice of what friends to make, whom to marry, what kind of government to elect – and, if we are fortunate enough, where to live, what kind of work to do, and what kind of school to send our children to. These are all choices of weight. Of less weight are choices between different kinds of material goods: different brands of coffee or soap powder, for example, or different makes of car. In the contemporary west we are now thoroughly accustomed to having available a wide choice of consumer goods; and this does augment the quality of life. It permits us to refine our tastes, to express our individuality more precisely, to enjoy the spice of variety and novelty.

Too wide a range of choice, however, can become oppressive. By nature humans want to make rational decisions; and this natural instinct is heightened and specified by the constant exhortations of commercial advertising urging us to consume more and more, and to make sure that we get value for money. Faced, then, with a wide array of goods to choose from, consumers who want to make rational choices are driven to devote enormous amounts of time and energy to making them. They are driven to spend a large part of their lives in making complicated choices about relatively trivial things.

According to the 'freedom to choose' ideology, living in North America should be a television consumer's delight. For, wherever you are, there are invariably dozens of TV channels to choose from, even if much of what they offer is virtually the same. But (at least in this author's experience) there comes a time when the prospect of having to set about the task of selecting the evening's viewing from the programmes of sixty television channels fills the soul with lead, and makes one yearn to be back in a country with only half-a-dozen. If it is good to be free to choose, it is equally good to be free from the burden of too much choice.

A second object for which we desire freedom, and which has already been alluded to, is the scope to discover and explore new things. Curiosity is a driving force in human life. As children we are naturally relentless in our questioning – unless our parents get tired or feel threatened and train us to regard our curiosity as impertinent. The human desire to know is as strong as, and not infrequently stronger than, the will to live. The human animal is not just concerned to fill its stomach, save its own skin, and reproduce itself in its offspring. Sometimes it is prepared to put all of these at risk for the sake of exploring the unknown, discovering the new, and comprehending the strange.

Not that our exploration is always intellectual. Greater understanding is not always what we are looking for. Sometimes what we are pursuing is heightened sensation, and our curiosity is aesthetic or sensual.

But sometimes what fuels our searching is not really curiosity at all, but anxiety. Sometimes we are desperate to explore uncharted territory just to distract us from a domestic challenge that we lack the courage to tackle, or to reassure ourselves that we are still capable of conquest. When men or women already committed to a relationship with one person find themselves compulsively flirting with others – and sometimes with utter strangers – it is often for reasons like these.

Beyond freedom to choose and to explore, we also want freedom to be or become ourselves. At its most degenerate this freedom for authenticity means nothing more than the freedom to do as we please. Here the self is identified with its prevailing moods and wants, and the freedom to be oneself amounts, ironically, to the 'freedom' to be driven by whatever appetites and aversions happen to be dominant. But according to a more dignified version, the freedom for authenticity regards the human individual as having unique possibilities to realize and a unique destiny to fulfil. This human being, with this inheritance, this history, this character, and these skills has an opportunity to achieve certain things in this place and at this time that no one else has, nor ever has had or will have in the history of the universe.

It is possible, of course, to achieve radically different kinds of things. One can bring about reconciliation between enemies or one can betray a friend. One can care for the poor or one can despise them. One can build or one can destroy. Through what I choose to intend and how I decide to act, I have the power to shape the world – and, with it, myself – uniquely for good or ill. My choices and decisions, then, are heavy with meaning. They matter.

But they matter only in so far as they presuppose some kind of given moral context or 'horizon', from which what I do and who I become derive their significance. As Charles Taylor, the Canadian philosopher, puts it:

> Even the sense that the significance of my life comes from its being chosen . . . depends on the understanding that *independent of my will* there is something noble, courageous, and hence significant in giving shape to my own life. There is a picture here of what human beings are like, placed between this option for self-creation, and easier modes of copping out, going with the flow, conforming with the masses, and so on, which picture is seen as true, discovered, not decided. Horizons are given.[2]

The freedom to be authentic, then, is not the 'freedom' to follow a whim or surrender to passion. Nor is it simply the freedom to be unique. Rather, it is the freedom to shape oneself as an individual in the course of fulfilling oneself as a human being; and that involves investing oneself in human goods by acting in their service, and thereby doing what is 'right'.

Such a moral understanding of authenticity might seem a bit odd, in that the freedom to be oneself is commonly assumed to involve the defiance of moral convention. This is because the contemporary ideal of the truly authentic individual is typically that of the Romantic genius whose inspired originality and creativity dispenses such a person from having to observe the small-minded regulations of 'morality'. Here, the freedom to become oneself is thought of precisely as the freedom to grow and to create *in spite of* normal moral rules.

In one important respect our understanding of authenticity agrees with this Romantic notion: that moral life is not just about keeping the rules. Moral life is not just about being respectable and conventional and safe. It is not just about making sure that we do not step out of line. It is not just about obedience. It is more challenging than that, more responsible, maybe more adventurous and heroic. Authentically moral individuals do not simply let the tide of convention carry them where it will. Their basic commitment is to the human good, not to the demands of social expectation. Moreover, they are aware that there do arise situations where given moral rules appear to require action that would harm, rather than serve, such good; and in these cases, they are willing to take the risk of questioning and reconsidering received moral wisdom.

But where this vision of the authentic self differs from the Romantic version is in the clear distinction it makes between what is truly moral and what is conventional. Genuine authenticity is always moral; it is about the individual's unique realization, in this particular place and at this particular time, of what is universally good, and thereby their becoming more fully human. If, in the process of doing this, authentic individuals dissent from moral convention, it is not because they are being immoral or because they think themselves to be 'beyond morality'. Nor is it because they are indulging themselves in playing the fashionable part of Rebel-Iconoclast. If they dissent, it is only because they think they have a better grasp than convention of what really is moral.

Truly authentic individuals, then, are not free in the sense of being a law unto themselves. Rather, they are free in that they have the power to create and complete themselves in the course of making their unique and intelligent response to the call of what is good.

What applies to authenticity, applies also to choice and exploration. Whatever our freedom is for, if it is to deserve the significance and value with which we instinctively accredit it, then it has to stand within a moral context. In itself, the freedom to choose can be overwhelming, oppressive, and paralysing; and the objects of choice can be worthless, even harmful. And the freedom to explore can be a pretext for running away from painful tasks, and so for letting slip precious opportunities to build and to grow. Therefore, if freedom *for* anything is to be valuable, it needs to take the basic form of a commitment to what is good.

And what is true of positive freedom must also be true of negative freedom; for the value of being free *from* anything is only that, as a consequence, we are then free *for* something else *worthwhile*. Freedom from an authority or a tradition, for example, is valuable in so far as it enables us to explore new ideas or adopt new practices; and such exploration and innovation are valuable only in the course of pursuing what is true and what is just.

Freedom finds its value in the service of human flourishing. Or not at all.

4

WORK
. . . ON NOT MAKING A TYRANNY
OUT OF A NECESSITY

> Living in the cold, hungry, dark city, people held themselves
> together by the consciousness of being needed. They began to
> die when they had nothing to do. Nothing-to-do was more
> terrible than a bombing raid.[1]

What the people of Leningrad had impressed upon them in
the extreme conditions of the two-and-a-half year siege by
Hitler's forces from 1941 to 1943, those of us who have been
unable to work for prolonged periods have caught a glimpse of.
The human need to be needed, to be useful, is more powerful
than the need to survive. In the end, what drives us is not so
much the fear of death, as the fear of having nothing to build,
nothing worthwhile to contribute, nothing valuable to give.
Without a useful and valued role to play, mere existence loses
its appeal. Life becomes a kind of hell, every empty day taunt-
ing us with our meaninglessness. In these circumstances, death
comes to look very much like relief. Hence the correlation
between the recent rise in the rate of suicide among young
males in Britain and long-term unemployment.[2]

Work, then, seems to be a vital ingredient of human well-
being. Sometimes, it can even make us ecstatic. We can give
ourselves over to our work, become totally absorbed by it, be
driven by it, eat, drink and sleep it. The epitome of the man
(yes, typically a man) possessed by his work is the artistic genius

who, for days on end, does not think to stop for meals or sleep while labouring to give birth to the child of his creative inspiration. But there are plenty of more mundane, less Romantic examples, of the power of work to take hold of us and bear us away – examples of business people or financiers, academics or journalists, lawyers or doctors who live for their work.

From where does work get its ecstatic power, its power to transfix our attention on the task before us? Immediately, this comes from the tremendous 'buzz' it can give those who serve it. Work can be deeply exciting. This is the excitement of responding to a challenge. Faced with a puzzle to solve or a problem to unravel, our adrenalin starts to pump through our veins. The risk of failure and the lure of victory together bring us to the very edge of our seats and make us taut and alert with nervous energy. We are on an adventure, drawn by the possibility of gain, spurred on by the fear of loss. We are fully engaged in the venture of creation, fully launched on the journey of discovery. We are *alive*.

But work not only excites. It also exhilarates. This is the exhilaration of success. The sense of joy that, having taken the risks, having foregone the distractions of eating and sleeping, having concentrated our energies, having gathered ourselves – body, mind, and spirit – and engaged without reserve, we have won through. We have solved the puzzle. Unravelled the knot. Negotiated the peace. So: the thrill of victory; the elation of achievement.

Still, the exhilaration of work is not all about achievement. What exhilarates is not entirely the sight of the finished product. Indeed, it is not at all uncommon for that sight to disappoint. Success is often experienced as an anticlimax. No sooner have we got in our grasp what we have been chasing for months or years, than we find ourselves restlessly looking around for the next goal to pursue. What exhilarates, then, may well have less to do with the extrinsic result of our work, than with the intrinsic satisfactions of working. Regardless of the outcome of our efforts, there is the pleasure of being galvanized, being geared up. The deep satisfaction of exercising our powers as fully as we can. This is why it is possible to lose a game or a race and still to be exhilarated by it. We lost, but we played hard and to the best of our abilities. We held nothing back. We were entirely *there*.

However, having said all this, we should take care not to romanticize work. Some work is sheer labour; and all work is sometimes laborious. What makes it laborious is not just that it is physically demanding. Indeed, it need not be physically demanding at all. No, what makes it laborious is more its unrelenting homogeneity and repetitiveness, its endless tedium. Doing the same simple, undemanding operation again and again and again. Hour after hour. Day after day. Doing something that requires no imagination and little or no thought. Something that affords no scope for discretion, no room for the exercise of responsibility. Something that could be done as well by a machine as by a human being. Some kinds of work enable us to grow in our personal powers and in our humanity. Others stifle and deaden us.

Not that the quality of work is entirely intrinsic. For it is usually determined in part by its social context. The work itself may not excite us, but the company of those we work with might. Or our own little work may transcend its intrinsic tedium by bathing in the glow of significance that emanates from some larger, socially meaningful project to which it contributes. Even labour can be somewhat satisfying, if we believe it to be socially useful; and especially if others recognize it as such.

The problem, however, is that labour is more often taken-for-granted than appreciated. As the journalist, Martin Leighton, found out when he experimented with life as a streetsweeper in a British city in the early 1980s:

> I . . . quickly discovered my new status was that of a non-person, like an untouchable in India, a black in South Africa. People simply did not see me any longer. I felt that, but for the physical problem of mass, they would have walked through me. People would dump their filth where I had just swept, and some actually walked through newly-swept piles of rubbish and kicked them to the four winds.[3]

Why does labour tend to become invisible? In part, because it is not very interesting; for it does not involve eye-catching displays of human powers. In part, because it is usually devoted simply to maintaining the world, keeping the machine of ordinary life ticking over, rather than improving or embellishing it. But, perhaps most of all, it goes unappreciated because, if those whose work depends on other people's labour were to give it due credit, they would be strongly pressed to recognize their own obligation either to do more of it themselves, or to reward those who already do it more generously.

But the social pressure to leave the boring, obscure, laborious tasks to someone else is very strong. Social esteem accrues to those who strut across the public stage. Traditionally, men – and now increasingly women, too – measure their own worth according to their *public* productivity. What really matters is what we do in the office. What really matters is what we do 'at work' – as managers or salespeople, writers or clergy. This is where we are led to expect to win our sense of self-worth and of being valuable. Which is why being made redundant or retiring can be so devastating.

The strong drive to be successful 'at work' inclines us to neglect the non-professional dimensions of our lives. It encourages us to demean the workaday tasks that have to be undertaken if those dimensions are to flourish: the giving of time and attention to the care of the young and the infirm, the nurturing of a marriage, the cultivation of friendship, and the fulfilment of neighbourhood responsibilities. We tend not to grace these activities with the status of 'work'. They do not contribute to our careers. They do not help to make us 'successful'. So we brush them aside as distractions.

For a vivid illustration of this, take a dream that came to me some years ago. In this dream, I'm in the vestry of a church. And I'm pacing up and down in a state of intense agitation. I have a sermon to deliver, you see, but I can't figure out how to conclude it, and the service is about to begin. Then I notice at the back of the room, lounging by the door, a drunk. He's got fair hair and a beard, both thick with sweat and dirt. He's wearing a battered tweed hat, pale green. He stinks of sweat and booze and, worst of all, he's babbling incessantly at the top of his slurred voice. My patience is close to breaking; it's almost time to mount the pulpit, and I still haven't finished my sermon. Intense with irritation I shout at him to be quiet, but he ignores me. That does it. I walk over to him, raise my fists, and bring them down on his head, again and again and again, until I've beaten him into silence . . .

It's good to want to do good work. It's good to want to perform well. It's good to want to achieve what we're capable of achieving – whether it's a good degree, a successful career, an important piece of research, or a flourishing enterprise. It's good to have ambitions, to be determined to advance from A to B. But we must be careful not to be too determined, or we'll find ourselves behaving like the priest and the Levite who, in their haste to get from Jerusalem to Jericho on business that was doubtless as important as it was urgent, walked right past the humane and humanizing work of compassion:

> Jesus replied, 'A man was going down from Jerusalem to Jericho, and he fell among robbers, who stripped him and beat him, and departed, leaving him half dead. Now by chance a priest was going down that road; and when he saw him he passed by on the other side. So likewise a Levite, when he came to the place and saw him, passed by on the other side. But a Samaritan, as he journeyed, came to where he was; and when he saw him, he had compassion, and went to him and bound up his wounds, pouring on oil and wine; then he set him on his own beast and brought him to an inn, and took care of him . . .'[4]

Not that we always dismiss the demands of domestic care as distractions. Sometimes, if we are men, we just dismiss them (albeit unconsciously) as 'woman's work'. This, in spite of the historic shift that is taking place in our culture away from the traditional division of labour – between domestic work undertaken by women, and predominantly full-time paid work undertaken by men.[5] More and more women are entering paid employment – for the intellectual stimulation, the company, the independence and the money. In 60 per cent of couples both partners now have jobs – an increase of 17 per cent in 20 years.[6] However, in spite of the fact that most male partners affirm equality between the sexes in principle, the division of domestic labour appears to remain highly inequitable in practice. According to the report, *British Social Attitudes 1991*, in dual-earner families where both men and women work full-time, women are still mainly responsible for domestic duties in 67 per cent of households.[7] And according to *Life at 33*, a survey published in 1993, although 69 per cent of the sample said that men should do the same tasks as women around the house, in fact in 77 per cent of cases women did the cooking, 66 per cent the shopping, 75 per cent the cleaning, and 85 per cent the laundry.[8] This UK survey produced similar results to US studies which have found that, although women tend to spend fewer hours in paid employment, once their domestic work is taken into account, they can be seen to work an extra 15 unpaid hours per week, amounting to an extra 1 month's work per year.[9]

This inequity has two damaging social effects. First, as a major cause of discontent among women, it adds to the strains suffered by many marriages.[10] Second, since the movement of women out of the home and into the workplace has not yet been matched by a redirection of male energies from the workplace back into the home, a 'care-deficit' has opened up. Fewer women are now available to provide the informal care of children, relatives and neighbours than was the case in the past, and their male partners are not (as a rule) exactly queuing up to fill the domestic vacuum.[11]

There is an urgent social need, then, for second thoughts about what constitutes valuable work. We need to re-evaluate and upgrade the worth of all the obscure, laborious work that goes into bringing up children, nursing grandparents, and helping to run the local fête. It needs to be recognized as vital for social well-being – as a vital contribution to the commonwealth. It needs to be recognized as such by men, by employers, and by Government. And recognition here needs to reach beyond verbal commendation. If we really recognize 'care in the community' as a very valuable kind of socially useful work, then presumably we would be loathe to see those who undertake it suffer economic penalties for their pains. Indeed, we should want to see them encouraged, if not rewarded. If those who make things or make money, or those who administer public services, keep the peace, teach the young, and heal the sick, deserve status and rewards, then surely those who privately nurse infants or the infirm, day and night, deserve adequate support – at the very least?

Part of what our re-evaluation of work should involve is an extension of our concept of useful work. Useful work is not just what goes on in the workplace; but also what goes on in the home and the neighbourhood. It's not just about making things and money (important though these might be); it's also about caring for people and building friendship.

However, we need to do more than just extend our concept of usefulness. We need to expand our concept of work itself. We tend to think of work as activity that brings about effects in the world; that is, in the world *out there*. Work lays bricks, types letters, nurses patients, designs computer programs, sells commodities, writes books, cures people of disease. But there is another kind of work – or, better, another dimension of it. There is also the work that brings about effects in the world *in here*; that is, in the person who is working. Indeed, every act we perform shapes us as well as the rest of the world. In every act we make ourselves, we build and modify our character, augment or diminish our strengths and weaknesses. What we do today helps to determine the qualities we take with us into tomorrow, and so the range of possibilities that we are capable of realizing. And just as our work can cause things out there to work well or badly, so they can cause things in here. So the happiness that we derive from our work is not simply on account of our being instruments of good in the world. It is not simply on account of our being useful to other people. What makes us even more deeply happy – what gives us joy – is being ourselves in the state of working well. Not just working well as a nurse or sales assistant or manager or farmer or teacher or mother. Not just working well in our various social and economic roles. But working well as a human being. This is the point that T. H. White was making when he wrote:

> Imagine a rusty bolt on the garden door, which has been set wrong, or the door has sagged on its hinges since it was put on, and for years that bolt has never been shot efficiently: except by hammering it, or by lifting the door a little, and wriggling it home with effort. Imagine then that the old bolt

is unscrewed, rubbed with emery paper, bathed in paraffin, polished with fine sand, generously oiled, and reset by a skilled workman with such nicety that it bolts and unbolts with the pressure of a finger – with the pressure of a feather – almost so that you could blow it open or shut. Can you imagine the feelings of the bolt? They are the feelings of glory which convalescent people have, after a fever. It would look forward to being bolted, yearning for the rapture of its sweet, successful motion. For happiness is only a bye-product of function, as light is a bye-product of the electric current running through the wires. If the current cannot run efficiently, the light does not come. That is why nobody finds happiness, who seeks it on its own account. But man must seek to be like the working bolt; like the unimpeded run of electricity; like the convalescent whose eyes, long thwarted in their sockets by headache and fever, so that it was a grievous pain to move them, now flash from side to side with the ease of clean fishes in clear water. The eyes are working, the current is working, the bolt is working. So the light shines. That is happiness: working well.[12]

What is it, then, to work well as a human being? That is, what does human flourishing consist in? One answer, implied in Chapter Two, is that working well as a human being consists fundamentally in acknowledging what is true, and aligning ourselves with it in what we say and what we do. And among the most important truths that we should acknowledge is this: that there are certain goods which deserve to be appreciated, maintained and promoted. Working well as a human being, then, involves recognizing goods and investing ourselves in caring for them, even though it cost us dear.

One practical consequence of this understanding of good work is that human life does not cease to have value when it ceases to be 'useful'. Human beings who have ceased to be capable of 'productive' work – whether through physical or mental infirmity – do not thereby cease to be valuable. They may not be able to clean, cook, build, manage or compose. They may be confined to a bed or a wheelchair. They may even be comatose. But they are still capable of acknowledging the goods of friendship and community by exhibiting care for others, even if only in the reduced form of accepting care from them. And maybe this manner of care is not really 'reduced' at all. For it is no small service to appreciate the value of what others have to give, even when one's appreciation is restricted to the basic form of just letting them give it. Perhaps we love others, above all, when we welcome their love for us.

But there is another important truth to which those who are infirm can bear witness; namely, that human powers are limited. By accepting, with a measure of grace, that they cannot do everything, that they cannot do all that they had hoped and planned to do, that they cannot do most of what they used to do, that they cannot do much at all, the infirm acknowledge their natural status as beings of limited power. And in so doing they perform the valuable work of affirming an important truth. It is an important truth because those who deny it end up injuring those around them.

We are limited in our power to guarantee the results of our efforts, the achievement of our work. We cannot be sure of sufficient time to start what we intend or to finish what we have started. At any moment, other more urgent claims of life, or some kind of suffering, or death itself may interrupt our progress, perhaps forever. An ancient Jewish sage once put it in this way:

> Again I saw that under the sun the race is not to the swift, nor the battle to the strong, nor bread to the wise, nor riches to the intelligent, nor favour to the men of skill; but time and chance happen to them all. For man does not know his time. Like fish which are taken in an evil net, and like birds which are caught in a snare, so the sons of men are snared at an evil time, when it suddenly falls upon them.[13]

But our achievement is uncertain in another sense, too; in that we cannot tell what it is worth, except in the most relative of terms; and even if its effects were unambiguously good, we still could not predict the extent or the duration of their influence. The destiny of our efforts is quite obscure to us. Our sage, again:

> I hated all my toil in which I had toiled under the sun, seeing

that I must leave it to the man who will come after me; and who knows whether he will be a wise man or a fool? Yet he will be master of all for which I toiled . . .[14]

One possible reaction to the fragility and ambiguity of human achievement is to despair, to throw up our hands and exclaim, 'Why bother? Why strive? What's the point? If, in the end, all is reduced to dust, why should we take the trouble to build? Or, at least, why should we take the trouble to build beyond what is necessary to diminish our pain and increase our pleasure?'

Against reacting in this way, there are a number of considerations. One is that, although our ability to achieve what we intend may be limited and the destiny of our achievement uncertain, that does not mean that we will not realize our intentions or that our achievement will not promote what is good down the whole length of history. Just because we cannot be absolutely sure does not warrant our taking refuge in the false certainty of despair. The awareness that we are not Masters of the Universe is cause for humility, not sulkiness.

Further, the achievement of our work is subjective as well as objective: we build ourselves as well as a world. And, unless we are certain that death is the end of us absolutely, unless we are certain that the souls we have made of ourselves could not be fit to live and flourish for ever, there remains the possibility that what we have built well will, in the end, amount to considerably more than a pile of dust.

Third, the intrinsic satisfaction we experience when engaged in building what is good, suggests a profound, instinctive faith in the worthwhileness of what we are doing. This satisfaction is not just an instance of whistling heroically in the howling darkness; for whereas the tragic whistling hero is half-aware of the groundless artificiality of his confidence – hence the forced quality of his whistling – those who are involved in doing good work experience contentment or exhilaration as something that comes upon them or wells up within, and not as something that they have to work up or engineer.

Finally, those who commit themselves to doing good work in spite of uncertainty, and even in spite of adversity and failure, are seen by their neighbours to shine; whereas those who retreat into the miserable comforts of despair become beclouded, and they envelop in shadow whatever and whomever crosses their path.

Despair, however, is only one possible reaction to the fragility and uncertainty of human work. Another is sheer denial. To refuse to accept the limits of human power. To become absolutely determined to succeed and to preserve one's achievement at all costs. To become monomaniacal, brooking no opposition, suffering neither fools nor the weak, meeting the threat of failure only with mounting ruthlessness.

But this is unrealistic, because maximal ruthlessness is still a long way short of a guarantee of success. And, besides, its effects are bound to be destructive, both of the world and of the person who brings them about. For ruthless means cannot *really* serve worthwhile ends. Revolutionary terror, for example, cannot be made to grow the seeds of fraternity, but only those of fear, suspicion, treachery, grievance and vengeance.

It is possible, however, to respond to the uncertain and precarious nature of human work and achievement with neither despair nor ruthlessness, but only humility. It is possible to remain committed to building what is good in spite of its vulnerability. To be patient and resilient when our efforts fail, refusing to do evil in order to save the day, but picking ourselves up off the ground and starting again. It is possible to acknowledge our duty to try, without claiming any right to succeed.

Whether the strengths of character necessary for such conduct are sustainable without a measure of religious faith is open to question. How, without the support and constraint of some faith in the active presence in the world of a more-than-human, benevolent, and perhaps supreme, power, it is possible *both* to admit the feebleness or ineffectuality of our efforts to stem evil or advance good, or to watch helplessly the crumbling and collapse of our achievements, *and still* to resist the allurements of despair and ruthlessness, is not obvious. And even if it were possible, how much sense would it make?

5

ECSTASY
. . . RISING UP, MOVING OUT,
AND CONNECTING

Ecstasy is the name of a popular drug.

It is also the name of a popular state of consciousness.

The word 'ecstasy' is an English form of the Greek original, *ekstasis*, meaning literally 'an out-standing'. It refers to a state of consciousness where one is aware of standing outside of oneself, of being beside oneself. But not merely a standing outside. Also a rising above. For ecstasy involves a sense of elation, of uplift, of being disencumbered, of buoyancy, of joy. A sense of transcending normal limitations.

The drug that borrows its name from the mental state does so because it induces an overwhelming sense of empathy or fellow-feeling for other people. It breaks down the normal barriers to communication – the fears of being rejected, exposed, humiliated or manipulated – and enables the loss of socially inhibiting self-consciousness. Not all 'recreational' drugs have such sociable effects. Marijuana, for example, causes consciousness to be totally absorbed by a particular thing – a colour, a sensation, a word – and to lose its grip on larger wholes. It tends, therefore, to inhibit communication. Try saying something of sentence-length when you're 'stoned', and you will find yourself petering out mid-way, because your attention has been so absorbed by a fragment – a word or syllable – that you have lost all track of what went before and what was intended to follow after. Marijuana is myopic, not ecstatic. It causes the self to collapse inward, not to expand outward. 'Ecstasy' does the reverse.[1]

A less artificial and expensive way of achieving ecstasy is, of course, sex. And, since sex became more readily available and less fraught with possible complication for western people, thanks to the mass production of contraceptives and the subsequent revolution of attitudes in the 1960s, it has become the most common way. Some might think that to describe sex as a route to ecstasy is to take it far too seriously, to exaggerate its significance, to romanticize it. For surely, they might say, sex is just a matter of satisfying certain physical desires, like eating or defecating or scratching an itch; ecstasy is far too grand and inflated an end for it.

It may be that for some people sex seems as simply physical as this. But it seems reasonable to ask why, if that is so, we tend to seek sexual pleasure with other persons. Healthy adults do not need help to eat or defecate or scratch themselves. So why do we usually want sex to be sociable, not solitary? Why are we inclined to regard masturbation as second-best? One retort might be that sociable sex is more physically pleasurable. But why should that be? There are not many erogenous zones of one's own body that one's own hands cannot reach. And the heightened and more satisfying pleasure of sociable sex is surely not entirely attributable to the element of surprise in the unpredictable movements of another pair of hands? So, if sex is simply a matter of physical pleasure, why is it qualitatively better when done with another person?

The answer is that sexual desire, at least when it has matured beyond early adolescence, is desire, not merely for physical satisfaction, but for intimate personal communion. It is not enough that we are touched by another's hands; for if the other person ignores our needs or fears, or if they threaten us, their touch will not be experienced as pleasure. No, we want to be touched by hands and lips that care, that are aware of us and respond to us – as persons, not just as bodies. We want them to be expressive of love. Or, to be more precise, we want them to belong to someone who loves us. Usually, we do not want to have sex with just anybody – except, perhaps, when we misread sexual desire as desire for physical satisfaction simply. Usually, we want to have sex with someone in particular, someone who cares for us – or, at least, someone whom we can *imagine* cares for us. We want to be able to step over our defences, rise above our inhibitions, and give ourselves without reserve, confident that what we give will not be spurned or ridiculed.

Sexual desire is the desire for ecstasy. The desire to break out of the bounds of one's own skin and to be welcomed through the bounds of another's. The desire to be out of one's own control and yet held by another. Indeed, it is precisely on account of its ecstatic intention that Western Christian culture has tended to be suspicious of sexual desire as such. Its dominant view of this matter, as of much else, was decisively shaped by St Augustine, bishop of Hippo in North Africa early in the fifth century AD. Augustine, whose early adulthood seems to have been driven by vain attempts to appease an insatiable libido,[2] later found anchorage partly in the Stoic ideal of human dignity as consisting in rational self-control. On the one hand, this ideal promised relief from the miserable tyranny of sexual obsessiveness. But on the other hand, it led Augustine – and most of the Western Christian tradition in his wake – to regard the supremely ecstatic moment of orgasm, and the desire that intends it, as the epitome of sinfulness. Hence his unhappy and fateful doctrine of the original sin of Adam and Eve being transmitted from generation to generation through the very act of sexual intercourse.[3]

However, Augustine was mistaken to suppose that sexual ecstasy is simply a loss of rational self-control; that is, a loss of control in which we abandon our peculiarly human qualities and start behaving like animals. After all, it is not as if we fall unconscious when we become sexually active. We know what we are doing. We have reasons for doing it. We intend something by it. Indeed, the more skilled we are at heightening and prolonging sexual pleasure, the more controlled and deliberate our actions will be; and, since one of the most potent sources of sexual stimulation is awareness of success in giving pleasure to one's partner, the greater our sexual skill is, the greater will be our sensitivity and responsiveness to the other person.

The 'loss of control' involved in sexual ecstasy is not the same as that in going beserk or running amok. It is far more like the 'loss of control' involved in dancing. The actions of a dancer are not chaotic or disordered. Quite the contrary: the better a dancer, the more ordered the movements. But dancing does require the loss of a certain kind of self-consciousness. A ceasing to care what other people think about our performance. Or, perhaps better, a confidence that, even if we do seem to others to be clumsy and uncool, they will still respect us enough not to ridicule or despise us. Either way, whether through sheer self-confidence or confidence in others, good dancing requires us to be free to take our mind off ourselves and how we appear and whether others approve, and to focus instead on the music. It requires us to be free to pay attention to it, to follow it, to give ourselves over to it. A good dancer is able to let the dance play her. Likewise, a good lover.

Older people might assume that the younger generation's attitude to sex and drugs is one of sheer hedonism: the pursuit of sensual pleasure, simply. The recent growth in popularity of rave culture suggests otherwise. Raves are all-night events, held either out in the open air or in vast warehouses, at which hundreds or thousands of young people dance to music with a heavy, driving beat and almost no melody. The effect of prolonged periods of raving is ecstatic: it produces feelings of elation and empathy. Some ravers seek to intensify the effect by taking Ecstasy. But many do not; and there is evidence that the ecstatic feelings of those who are not drugged are actually greater. The loud, relentless beat and the collective energy are effective enough by themselves.[4] What is perhaps more remarkable is that the satisfaction produced by raving seems equal, if not superior, to the satisfaction of sex. Sexual activity is not, in fact, a major feature of raves, even though they gather together masses of young men and women, many of them scantily dressed, in close physical proximity, and in semi-darkness. This suggests that when one male raver frankly confessed to a TV reporter that, in his experience, raving was far better than sex, he was not just speaking for himself.[5]

One of the features of the rave that helps to inspire ecstasy is its corporate nature. The same young man who rated it better than sex implied that what is better about it is the sense of belonging to a corporate self. As is now well recognized, a crowd is more than a collection of individuals. It has a psyche of its own into which it has the power to absorb the individual

psyches of its members. Individuals who by themselves are normal enough human beings and decent enough citizens, can go
beserk when part of an enraged mob. They become beside
themselves with collective rage. This is another way of achieving ecstasy, and one which some prefer. Hence the attraction
of being a football hooligan and belonging to one of the various
'firms' or gangs which engineer vicious battles with their rivals,
whether on the terraces, in the streets, in subway stations, or in
railway carriages. Looking back nostalgically on his days in the
now-disbanded Subway Army,[6] Tony tries to explain the thrill
of mob violence: 'It's just a buzz. A feeling of power. Knowing
you are with a bunch of geezers who can do another firm.'[7]
Kevin, life-long Spurs fan who was among those arrested during
clashes at the 1984 UEFA cup final at Anderlecht in Belgium,
brings out more clearly the reality of the corporate psyche: 'We
went out there and ran riot . . . We went mental. Everyone was
robbing people, attacking people on the street. It was a brilliant
laugh. There was a bond between us. If you were on your own
doing it, it wouldn't be the same. It's like tribal warfare.'[8] But it
is Bill Buford, a literary editor who spent eight years drinking,
marching, and eventually fighting with some of Britain's most
violent football thugs, who has managed to touch the heart of
the matter. His insight into the pull of mob violence was born
in the middle of a street-battle between Manchester United and
Chelsea fans in Fulham. He writes: 'I was on a druggy high, in
a state of adrenalin euphoria. And for the first time I am able
to understand the words they use to describe it. That crowd
violence was their drug. What was it like for me? An experience
of absolute completeness.'[9] And, recounting an earlier fracas in
Turin, Buford recalls that just as violence started to explode, a
mate said to him 'that he was very, very happy, that he could
not remember ever being so happy'.[10]

These testimonies to ecstasy as the point of mob violence are
corroborated by evidence that the decline of football violence
in the later 1980s was caused in part by the rise in rave culture.
As Tony wistfully said in 1993: 'Things have really quietened
down nowadays. Everybody's going to raves on a Friday night,
getting home at 7am – they've taken Ecstasy – they're not fit for
anything in the morning. Everyone's into peace and love and

all that bullshit.'[11] A rave, it seems, offers similar satisfactions to mob violence, but without the hassle.

There is, of course, a far more traditional means of achieving ecstasy, and one that is arguably as natural as sex: religion. Significantly, both Buford and the TV documentary, *Rave New World*, note the parallels between religious ecstasy and, respectively, crowd violence and raving. Indeed, Buford reports one of his mates as saying of football thuggery, 'It's a religion.' But what could he have meant by this? What could possibly be religious about being part of a violent mob or a raving crowd? Another of Buford's comrades spoke of being intensely happy. But what has that got to do with religion? The connection is suggested by Buford's own testimony to a sense of 'absolute completeness'. For, taken together with other testimonies to the corporate or tribal dimension of the experience, it indicates that the individual's intense feelings of well-being are a by-product of being a member of a larger whole. Individuals are not complete simply in themselves. They are complete in themselves because they are deeply connected to other people. They feel at rest in themselves precisely because they have moved out from themselves. They are fully themselves because they have become part of a social entity.

But it is not just the mere sense of social belonging that gives the ecstasy of mob violence or raving its religious quality. It is also the sense that the social body of which one is a member is endowed with absolute value. The raving crowd appears as an epiphany of Love; and the rioting mob, settling old scores, poses as an agent of Justice. The propensity of football hooliganism to take on nationalist overtones confirms this point. For nationalism is a kind of substitute-religion: with its roots in Time Immemorial, its historic mission to liberate or civilize or cleanse the world, and its destiny securely lodged in eternity, the Nation is effectively thought of as the embodiment of the divine Spirit; and members of this body, especially those who have sacrificed their lives for it, are assured of a kind of ersatz-immortality in the reverent memories of future generations where, as the war memorials promise, 'their name liveth for evermore'.[12] Football hooligans, especially those who give their tribal instinct nationalist expression, are able to locate themselves in the larger whole of what claims to be a universal drama of absolute significance. This, more than just corporate belonging, is what gives their ecstatic experience its religious quality.

Or, at least, its *quasi*-religious quality. I say this because the whole of which the football thug is a member is, in fact, only a limited whole. It is not really absolute or universal. Its cause cannot be equated with that of justice simply, if at all. Its destiny is not coterminous with the perfection of the whole human race. Its agency is not identical with God's. But the football 'firm', like all too many national tribes, has divine and imperial pretensions. Rather than acknowledge that it is but one among many, that it possesses vices as well as virtues, that it needs others to supply its weaknesses; rather than acknowledge its own finitude and imperfection, it pretends to be absolute and sets about trying to absorb everything else into itself, refashioning the whole world in its own image, subordinating the foreign to the familiar, the 'barbaric' to the 'civilized'.

Many religions support these pretensions. Their gods serve to absolutize a particular tribe, to divinize its social structure, its moral values, and its historic destiny. In many cases, Durkheim was quite correct: 'God' is the name we give to society, to the corporate psyche.[13]

But this is not true in all cases. There are some forms of religion that worship a God whom they understand to be supremely non-partisan. It is not just that this God is supposed to have jurisdiction over all things, but also that he does not govern all things in the interest only of some of them. His rule is characterized by justice for all.

Such a conception of God is characteristic of a certain tradition of Judaism, for example, whose holy scriptures include a substantial section entitled 'The Prophets'. This comprises the writings of men who, mostly between the eighth and the fifth centuries BC, *criticized* the tribes of Israel *in the name of their own God*. And among the things that they criticized was Israel's tribalism. Together with other Jews the prophets believed that Israel was a people specially chosen by God as the means by which the whole world would be saved from the ravages of sin and restored to health. But at the same time they denounced tendencies amongst their own people to presume upon their status; to assume that since they were the chosen – the elect – of God, he would sanction whatever they did to further their own interests. One of the prophets who was most bitter in his denunciation of religiously sanctioned tribalism was Amos. Amos was a shepherd from a small village in Judaea who lived during the reign of King Jeroboam II (c.786–c.746 BC), when Israel attained a degree of territorial expansion and national prosperity that it was never to surpass. Such national success was taken by many Israelites to be evidence of God's unconditional favour, something they felt they had earned by their extravagant support of official religious institutions. Probably at some point during the decade 760–750 BC, Amos felt called by God to gainsay such presumption. In God's name he denounced his own people, together with their pagan neighbours, for their social injustice, sexual immorality and religious hypocrisy:

> Thus says the Lord: 'For three transgressions ... and for four, I will not revoke the punishment; because they sell the righteous for silver, and the needy for a pair of shoes – they that trample the head of the poor into the dust of the earth, and turn aside the way of the afflicted; a man and his father go in to the same maiden ... ; they lay themselves down beside every altar upon garments taken in pledge; and in the house of their God they drink the wine of those who have been fined.'[14]

The fact that a people has been called by God to play a special, even a unique, part in the drama of the salvation of the world, does not, according to Amos, mean that it is given *carte blanche* to do as it pleases. Nor does it mean that its part is the only one to be played:

> 'Are you not like the Ethiopians to me, O people of Israel?' says the Lord. 'Did I not bring up Israel from the land of Egypt, and the Philistines from Caphtor and the Syrians from Kir?'[15]

This Jewish tradition of prophetic anti-tribalism was continued by Jesus and developed by St Paul into one of the distinctive features of nascent Christianity. A constant refrain in Jesus' ministry is his denunciation of the mean fastidiousness and lack of compassion of some of the forms of religion dominant among his own people; and there are several stories in the Gospels where Jesus recognizes genuine religious faith in non-Jews.[16] This tendency, evident in Jesus, to recognize that true religiosity transcends ethnic boundaries was developed by Paul, who argued that to be a genuine child of Abraham, the progenitor of the Jewish people, one must share his faith in God but not necessarily his blood. The people of God comprise all who have such faith, regardless of race, social class or sex. Therefore, wrote Paul famously, 'There is neither Jew nor Greek, there is neither slave nor free, there is neither male nor female.'[17]

The general point being made here is that not all forms of religion are tribalist. Some may be essentially so, and others become so in spite of themselves – for example, instances of Roman Catholic and Orthodox Christianity in the former Yugoslavia, and Roman Catholic and Protestant Christianity in Northern Ireland. Nevertheless, there are forms of religion that are constitutionally anti-tribalist, and whose God seeks the good of all things, the common good, and not just the partial good of a few of them. These forms are the real thing, because they do not arbitrarily absolutize an imperfect part. Instead, they draw individuals out of themselves and into membership of a community that, recognizing the difference in power and virtue between itself and God, is thereby prepared to play its role, limited but significant, in the divinely driven drama of universal salvation.

Football thuggery (and nationalism and other tribalisms) are quasi-*religious* because they connect the individual with what pretends to be an absolute and perfect whole. But it is not the nature of the whole alone that warrants their being described as religious. There is also the fact that the supposed connection enlivens individual members. It invigorates. It exhilarates. It makes them feel truly alive, as if for the first time. It makes them feel that *this* is what it's all about. Whereas before life plodded along, now it soars. Ecstasy is not just about being moved *out of oneself*. It is also about being *moved* out of oneself.

This dynamic quality of ecstasy is arrestingly brought out in

Peter Shaffer's play, *Equus*. Alan Strang, an adolescent stable-boy, is brought to Martin Dysart, a psychiatrist, after being convicted of blinding six horses with a metal spike. As Dysart explores what happened and why, he discovers that Alan had developed an idiosyncratic religion whose object of worship is Equus – or, Horse. Equus seems to symbolize a combination of two kinds of religion: the ascetic and the erotic. On the one hand, Equus is a kind of Jesus-figure, somehow offering salvation by suffering a Passion of enslavement and humiliation. But, on the other hand, he represents the power of erotic and religious self-transcendence into a larger union. At one point Dysart asks Alan, 'What does he [Equus] say to you?'

Alan: 'I see you.' 'I will save you.'
Dysart: How?
Alan: 'Bear you away.' 'Two shall be one.'[18]

Then, later, Alan relives and describes one of his rites of worship when, at the stroke of midnight, he would take one of the horses from the stables where he worked, lead him down to a special field – the Field of Ha Ha! – caress him, feed him a lump of sugar, and then ride him naked into the night:

Alan: I'm stiff! Stiff in the wind!
My mane, stiff in the wind!
My flanks! *My* hooves!
Mane on my legs, on my flanks, like whips!
Raw!
Raw!
I'm raw! Raw!
Feel me on you! *On* you! *On* you! *On* you!
I want to be *in* you!
I want to BE you forever and ever! —
Equus, I love you!
Now! —
Bear me away!
Make us One Person![19]

Dysart is well aware that Alan's religion is in part the product of a sexual repression bequeathed him by his puritanical parents. He is also aware that Equus is a jealous god, whose oppressive and intrusive tyranny has provoked the boy into his rebellious act of terrible violence. Nevertheless, Dysart cannot stop himself from envying Alan. And what he envies is his ecstasy:

> The thing is [says Dysart] I'm desperate. You see, I'm wearing that horse's head myself. That's the feeling. All reined up in old language and old assumptions, straining to jump clean-hoofed on to a whole new track of being I only suspect is there. I can't see it, because my educated, average head is being held at the wrong angle. I can't jump because the bit forbids it, and my own basic force – my horse-power, if you like – is too little.[20]
>
> But that boy has known a passion more ferocious than I have felt in any second of my life. And let me tell you something: I envy it . . .
>
> Without worship you shrink . . . I shrank my *own* life. No one can do it for you. I settled for being pallid and provincial, out of my own eternal timidity . . . I tell everyone Margaret [Dysart's wife] is the puritan, I'm the pagan. Some pagan! Such wild returns I make to the womb of civilisation. Three weeks a year in the Peloponnese, every bed booked in advance, every meal paid for by vouchers, cautious jaunts in hired Fiats, suitcase crammed with Kao-Pectate! Such a fantastic surrender to the primitive. And I use the word endlessly: 'primitive'. 'Oh, the primitive world,' I say. 'What instinctual truths were lost with it!' And while I sit there . . . , that freaky boy tries to conjure the reality! I sit looking at pages of centaurs trampling the soil of Argos – and outside my window he is trying to *become* one, in a Hampshire field![21]

Dysart envies Strang as one who plods envies him who gallops. Dysart, too, yearns to be borne away, 'to jump clean-hoofed on to a whole new track of being'. He yearns for his pedestrian, suburban life to come alive with ecstasy. He yearns to be infused with a larger, more intense energy; to be bound to that which will not fade, but will tranfuse his life with the blood of everlasting significance.

Don't we all?

But there are different ways, and there are different destinations. There are easy ways to ephemeral ecstasies. We can go to bed with a lover and assuage our emptiness and loneliness for a while. We can buy drugs or entry to a rave, and with it a night's worth of universal empathy. We can lose ourselves in all-embracing sensation. But then what? Come the cold light of day, what have we gained? How have we grown? What more do we have to offer? Are we more disposed to keep giving when it starts to hurt? Are we better able to negotiate our way through deeply entrenched resentments and prejudices to a just peace? Have we grown in patience and perseverance and care and generosity? Or have we just escaped from the pain of responsibility into a moment of feeling-good?

Sex and drugs, of course, are not the only short-cuts to pseudo-ecstasy. Religion can be, too. Sometimes certain states of consciousness – feelings of peace or joy or expansiveness – become the main point of religious life for some religious people, for whom participation in rites of worship that kindle such feelings is the heart of their religious practice. Sometimes the whole of religious life is collapsed into moments of intense experience. In which case, it is hard to distinguish between the pious worshipper and the raver: for both are seeking to escape into the state of 'feeling-good'.[22]

Some kinds of ecstasy are ephemeral distractions from responsibility. Others are positively destructive. The yearning for ecstasy is what makes sense of much apparently 'mindless' violence. It is 'mindless' only to those who think in pedestrian terms. Only to those for whom intelligible violence must either be about interpersonal anger, class resentment, or adding to the stock of one's visible assets. In these terms, however, the violence of football thugs makes no sense. Its victims are usually strangers, and its perpetrators are not primarily out to rob. What is more, the thugs do not necessarily belong to the underclass of socially and economically deprived; it has been noted that many members of 'firms' hold down decent, well-paying jobs, and can afford to kit themselves out in expensive designer clothes. But revenge or material gain are not the only possible objects of violence. There is also the intrinsic object of the feeling of ecstasy that arises in the very course of its practice.

It is not very likely that those who have experienced the exhilaration of violence will be weaned off it by earnest appeals to decency, or even by threats of punishment. Violence, after all, gives (a sort of) *life*. Social respectability is hardly a substitute with strong appeal; and the immediate prospect of ecstasy might well seem worth the distant risk of punishment. It is quite understandable that those who feel that they have come alive through violence should not be willing to abandon it, except for something else that *vitalizes* – drug-taking, for example, or raving.

But is there no other way? Are the only forms of escape from the felt isolation and banality of normal life either ephemeral or destructive? Is there no ecstasy that both lasts and creates?

There is, but there are no short-cuts to it. The way leads back into daily life, and not away from it; past its surface and into its depths. It leads us to look upon those things that deserve our attention and care, and it moves us to embrace our responsibility for them. It brings us to secure ourselves in relationships of trust and generosity, rather than lose ourselves in corporate violence.

The way *is* the ecstasy; for the ecstasy is a practice – the ecstasy of the practice of love. A going out of the self to the other. A transcendence of the selfish self out of care for the other. A refusal to attend to the distracting voices of one's own appetites as they clamour for satisfaction, for the sake of heeding what the other has to say.

But this ecstatic love is not just a practice – though it is surely not less than that. It is also a power that can lift us up and bear us away. It is also a passion. In another of Peter Shaffer's plays, *The Gift of the Gorgon*, Edward Damson, passionate playwright of Slavo-Celtic blood, expounds the cleansing, cathartic virtue of the passion for revenge. This he does over and against liberal tolerance, which in his eyes is '[j]ust giving up with a shrug – as if you never really cared about the wrong in the first place . . . *Avoidance*, that's all it is! . . .'[23] But Helen, cool daughter of a liberal English academic and Edward's wife, retorts:

You go on about passion, Edward. But have you never realized there are many, many kinds? – Including a passion to kill our own passion when it's wrong . . . The truest, hardest, most adult passion isn't just stamping and geeing ourselves up. It's refusing to be led by rage when we most want to be . . . No other being in the universe can change itself by conscious will: it is *our privilege alone.* To take out inch by inch this spear in our sides that goads us on and on to bloodshed – and still make sure it doesn't take our guts with it.[24]

To give ourselves over to the passion of ecstatic love is to suffer a sometimes demanding discipline, which reaches its climax in the practice of forgiveness: the decision, made out of compassion and for the sake of a fruitful future, to absorb injury rather than retaliate. Nevertheless, and at the same time, it is also to come alive with the dignity and beauty of full humanity; a humanity that, if Christians are right, is graced with the ultimate ecstatic power:

. . . one of the soldiers pierced his [Jesus'] side with a spear;[25]

And Jesus said, 'Father, forgive them; for they know not what they do';[26]

Then Jesus . . . breathed his last;[27]

. . . The third day he rose again from the dead.[28]

6

TRIBAL LOYALTY
. . . CARING FOR THE TRIBE BY
LOOKING BEYOND IT

The key narrative of the new world order is the disintegration of national states into ethnic civil war; the key architects of that order are warlords; and the key language of our age is ethnic nationalism. With blithe lightness of mind, we assumed that the world was moving irrevocably beyond nationalism, beyond tribalism, beyond the provincial confines of the identities inscribed in our passports towards a global market culture which was to be our new home. In retrospect we were whistling in the dark. The repressed has returned, and its name is nationalism.[1]

Those of us who are citizens of western liberal democracies and who are employed, financially comfortable, and who may expect to rise socially and professionally as high as our talents merit, do not think of ourselves as belonging to a tribe. Being largely self-sufficient we tend to think of ourselves primarily as individuals and only secondarily, if at all, as members of a group. Tribes we regard as phenomena at home in the African bush or the Amazonian jungle, not in the cities and suburbs of Western Europe or North America. 'Tribal' behaviour characterizes primitive, uncivilized peoples. That is, *other* peoples.

Recent history, however, has been rather disturbing for us. The disintegration of Yugoslavia into an ethnic war of sometimes unbelievable savagery has brought 'tribalism' much closer to home. Guerrillas are mutilating corpses and snipers are shooting children in a Mediterranean country nearer to us than Greece; and the perpetrators of these atrocities are white caucasians, who come from what used to be one of the most prosperous and open parts of communist Europe.

The war in Croatia and Bosnia has made us realize that tribal violence is not the preserve of places like Rwanda. And the emergence of virulent and fascistic nationalisms out of the rubble of the former Soviet Union has shown us that the demons which kindled two World Wars in twentieth-century Europe were not, in fact, finally exorcized in 1945. So when we heard news reports of the latest bombing or killing in Northern Ireland and saw television footage of department stores engulfed in flame or of the blood-bespattered walls of the pub whose customers had been mown down by masked gunmen, we began to recognize the similarities between Belfast and Sarajevo or Beirut. It began to dawn on us that tribal warfare was not merely being waged on our front doorstep, but had been raging in the hall for some considerable time.[2]

Strange though it may seem, then, belonging to a tribe is highly valued even by some late-twentieth century westerners. Indeed, it is valued far more widely than we tend to suppose.

But what exactly is a tribe, and what does it mean to belong to one? For our purposes, we may define a tribe as a social group whose members are bound together by a strong sense of common interest and identity, and therefore by a strong sense of mutual loyalty. Tribes, then, may be formed by ties of blood, race, locality, language, social manners, economic or political interest, or religious conviction. They need not be bound together by a common place. There have been nomadic tribes since time immemorial; and nowadays there are tribes whose members are scattered world-wide.

In one sense, tribes are artificial, not natural. In spite of the stories they often tell themselves, their boundaries were not established by God and their roots do not go back to the beginning of time. Tribal identities are, to a considerable extent, constructed. The role of the mass circulation of newspapers, for example, in helping to create a sense of national community where none existed before, has been noted.[3]

Nevertheless, affection for one's tribe is perfectly natural. It is natural to care for the community that has nourished you, and that has, in so many respects, made you what you are. It is natural to identify with those who see the world in the same way as you do, who speak the same language, tell the same stories, admire the same heroes, value the same things. It is natural to feel drawn to those who reflect your own reading of reality and so confirm it as the right one. It is natural to love those with whom you can communicate easily, those whom you readily understand and by whom you are readily understood. It is natural to love your neighbour.

But we can say more than this. We can say not only that it is natural, but also that it is good. It is good to recognize how much of what you are and have depends upon what others have done or are doing. It is good to acknowledge your debts and to be grateful to your community and your predecessors for all that they have given you.

Furthermore, it is good to love your neighbour because, if you cannot love the one near to you, how can you expect to love someone far away? In one sense, of course, it is true that it is often easier to love at a distance. It is easier to love someone to whom you are not closely bound, someone who knows you little and upon whom you do not depend. It is easier, because there is less chance of being wounded or disappointed or exhausted or corrected — or of needing to be forgiven. But although it may be more demanding to love the neighbour – the one nearby – there is no other way of learning to love deeply. Charity begins somewhere close to home, or probably not at all.

But tribal loyalty is not only good as an expression of gratitude and of love for the neighbour. It is also good in so far as it involves commitment to certain values. Perhaps especially in the form of the modern nation, the tribe is seen by its members as 'standing for' such social values as liberty, equality and justice. Its identity has a definite moral dimension, which is exemplified in the paradigmatic events and heroes that are woven together into its official history, and which are commemorated by tribal monuments and rituals. Often these events will be moments of 'liberation from tyranny', or at least attempts at it – for the French, the Revolution of 1789; for Americans, the War of Independence; for Irish nationalists, the Easter Rising of 1916; for Ulster Protestants, the Battle of the Boyne in 1690; and for Britons, once upon a time the defeat of the Spanish Armada, but now the defeat of Hitler. And the heroes will often be champions of freedom or justice — for example, Abraham Lincoln, General de Gaulle, Winston Churchill, Mahatma Gandhi, Martin Luther King and Nelson Mandela. The formation of a tribe's identity is a fabrication in the sense that it is constructed out of a selective reading of history. But it is not necessarily a fabrication in the sense of being simply a pack of lies. Often it tells at least part of the truth, and that part which is morally inspiring.

Loyalty to a tribe is natural and good. But, as the twentieth century has taught us, it is easily corrupted. One agent of this corruption is arrogance. For in constantly confirming our reading of reality, tribal membership encourages us to forget that we are reading at all. Reality simply *is*. It is *there*. We do not read it; we *see* it. In belonging to a social group whose traditions and members constantly reflect and replay our own interpretations, we lose all awareness of the distinction between what is there and how we read it. Our basic (and questionable) assumptions become hidden from sight.

Tribal membership, then, can have the effect of closing our minds. It can move us to ignore or demean whatever is foreign and strange, to reject out of hand any criticism of 'our' ways of seeing or doing things. It can incline us to regard outsiders with contempt, to dismiss them simply as 'barbarians' – etymologically: those whose language, making no sense to us, must be nonsense. Tribal membership can make us arrogant and narrow-minded. And it can make us offensive. As witness this (ambiguous) comment by a Northern Irish Catholic priest to an English journalist:

> You look down on the Irish as figures of fun, stupid half-witted people of little or no account. Irish jokes, Irish jokes: sometimes we think that's all the British know about the Irish. Jokes about Paddy and his stupidity, how he cuts one end off a ladder to put it on the other to make it longer, and thousands more like that. The idea of the Irish as a cultured and civilised people is one that's hardly ever seemed to enter the British mind.[4]

The comment is ambiguous because it not only points out British tribal prejudice against the Irish, but also, ironically, is itself an instance of Irish tribal prejudice against the British. Is there really such a thing as 'the British mind'? Does it invariably despise the Irish? And do all or most Britons share in it?

Sometimes, of course, the denigration of others issues, not so much from a surfeit of self-confidence, as from a lack of it. In her study of the forging of British identity in the eighteenth and early-nineteenth centuries, Linda Colley has written:

> Imagining the French as their vile opposites, as Hyde to their Jekyll, became a way for Britons — *particularly the poorer and less privileged* — to contrive for themselves a converse and flattering identity. The French wallowed in superstition: therefore, the British, by contrast, must enjoy true religion. The French were oppressed by a bloated army and by absolute monarchy: consequently, the British were manifestly free. The French tramped through life in wooden shoes, whereas the British ... were shod in supple leather and, therefore, clearly more prosperous.[5]

It is one of the commonest devices for bolstering weak self-esteem: find someone to feel superior to, exaggerate their defects, and get others to join you. Then your superiority becomes a 'fact' – for, after all, the whole (of your limited) world affirms it!

The obverse of denigrating others, of course, is idealizing ourselves. And that means idealizing our past. Briege Duffaud offers a vivid instance of this in her fine novel, *A Wreath upon the Dead*. Here Marianne McLeod, the daughter of a Scottish landlord in the north of Ireland toward the middle of the nineteenth century, records in her diary a conversation with a native Irishman, Cormac O'Flaherty:

> Old Mr Hale has kindly provided a house in the village, at a peppercorn rent, to be transformed into a dispensary for the peasants ... Cormac O'Flaherty informs me that his family and neighbours view the idea with great enthusiasm, while naturally blaming the legendary callousness of foreign landlords for the lack of such a facility in the past. I rather tartly

enquired if, in the days of the native nobility he is always talking about, the country was overflowing with hospitals, schools, and an abundance of cheap food for the poor? He laughed and agreed that well no, those were shocking wild times, Miss McLeod, and the high-ups more interested in making war on one another, from what he'd heard. But, he said, there was nothing to complain about because at least the Gaels were free and among themselves, not dominated by strangers. I said sarcastically that I supposed he'd have *enjoyed* being a serf in a chieftain's army . . .[6]

To idealize our past requires us to forget much. And at this point the fabrication of our 'official' history becomes a less than innocent selection: not only are the noble moments highlighted, but the ignoble ones are suppressed. Take, for example, the historical memory of many Catholics in Northern Ireland, as observed by Fionnuala O'Connor:

> The MacMahons and the Duffins and others in Belfast taken away in the night by DI [District Inspector John W.] Nixon's soft-soled murder gang to die horribly on the side of the mountain: all this came early to many. But not the shooting of B Specials or police in Belfast, Fermanagh, south Derry; not the Protestant Donnelly children killed by a bomb thrown through their window after the MacMahon killings, and not the story of the seven Protestants, one a woman, only one a Special, taken from their homes and shot dead on the roadside at Altanaveigh in County Armagh (near the spot at Kingsmills where in 1976 ten Protestant workmen were taken from their minibus and killed by the IRA). Memories come filtered down the generations to leave only pure, distilled Catholic victimhood.[7]

This partisan editing of history is a problem. For by encouraging the tribe to see itself simply as blameless victim, possessed of the sole claim to right, it fosters intransigence and fuels conflict. It is not always motivated just by weak self-esteem. Sometimes it is driven by frustration at not having one's grievances heard. The stubborn deafness of those who refuse to acknowledge that they have done us wrong enrages us into an

obsessive recitation of the litany of injuries that we have suffered – and makes it very hard for us to admit the injuries that
we ourselves are responsible for inflicting. So is born the fruit-
less cycle of mutual recrimination.

And then frustration grows up into vengeance. The primitive rage for crude justice. The zeal to restore the balance by
creating an equality of suffering. Injuring the injurers. This,
too, can become the focus of tribal identity. A people can come
to define themselves mainly in terms of the injuries they – or
their ancestors – have suffered, and so identify themselves as
those committed to wreak revenge upon their ancient oppres-
sors. This is the mission that gives holy meaning to their lives.
This is their reason for living.

But vengeance is not a pretty sight. The injury that has con-
jured it may well have been grievous. The cry for redress may
be perfectly just. Anger at the impenitence of the wrongdoer
may be well deserved. But a face – whether of an individual or
a people – that is darkened by resentment and hatred is not
attractive. It inspires in onlookers not so much admiration as
pity. We may understand why a person or a people who have
been much battered and abused should be unable to grow
beyond their injury. We may sympathize with them. But we still
regard their inability as a failure. In the end, it signifies, not
strength, but weakness.

In *The Gift of the Gorgon*, referred to at the end of the previous chapter, Edward Damson represents the case for vengeance
against the case for forgiveness. On the one hand, he is
absolutely convinced that Clytemnestra was right to chop up
her husband, Agamemnon, for sacrificing their daughter: 'His
wife simply cleaned the slate. Sacrifice for sacrifice . . . That's
what bloodshed can do – clean things . . . Pure revenge . . .
means pure justice . . . There's only one real moral imperative:
don't piss on true rage – it can be the fire of sanity.'[8]

But Helen, his wife, objects vigorously that there are many
kinds of passion, and that 'the truest, hardest, most adult passion . . . [is] refusing to be led by rage when we most want to be.
That means every time a bomb goes off, yes, and every time a
baby is killed, and every other filthy thing that makes you sick
with fury. Stubbornly continuing to say No to blood.'[9]

77

In the end, Helen wins the argument by showing that it is forgiveness, not vengeance, that requires the greater strength and makes the greater peace. But there is a moment when, reacting spontaneously to a macabre trick that Edward has played on her, she stands on the very brink of taking revenge. What pulls her back are the words of her stepson, Philip: 'The truth is, you must forgive him or die.'[10]

Those who refuse to forgive, cease to live. They cease to live in the sense that they become unfree. They become immured in the past, chained to their loss, irrationally imagining that suffering inflicted on the one who injured them will somehow bring release. They become embittered, turned in upon themselves, twisted and darkened. They become barren, incapable of creating new life. They die because they repudiate the claims of love. They repudiate the call to grow up and outward into full humanity.

Those who refuse to forgive also tend to make themselves perpetrators of injury. This is partly because vengeance is seldom sufficiently self-controlled to take only its pound of flesh: usually it seizes more than its due. But the unforgiving also become injurers because, in order to stoke up the fires of their hatred, they have to demonize its object. They have to suppress awareness of any redeeming feature of their enemy, any extenuating and mitigating circumstance attending his crime, any hint of likeness between him and themselves. In some cases, no doubt, there may not be much to suppress. But in most cases there will be, and especially so at the corporate level. For here feelings of resentment and hatred, and the desire for revenge, become generalized. It is not just the individual perpetrator of the crime who is held guilty, but the group to which he belongs — his family, his people, his race, his nation. Even if the particular criminal is a raving psychopath with no sympathetic qualities whatsoever, it would be very unlikely that his people are exactly the same and deserve the same judgement. But hatred is seldom careful to discriminate. It equates Germans with Nazis, and Northern Irish Catholics with the IRA.

The untruthfulness and consequent unfairness of corporate hatred spreads across time as well as across space. The grandsons are condemned for their grandfather's crimes. So, in the eyes of the Serbian guerrilla, the Croatians in 1996 are indistinguishable from their fascist Ustashe forbears of fifty years ago. And in the eyes of many Northern Irish nationalists, the British squaddies patrolling the streets of west Belfast wear virtually the same boots as those of Cromwell's troops who hacked their way through women and children at Drogheda in 1649.

Tribal loyalty, which in itself is natural and good, is vulnerable to corruption. Arrogance, parochialism, insecurity, resentment, vengefulness – these are among the factors that can turn legitimate loyalty into a prejudice that vitiates the self and abuses others.

So far, our discussion of tribal loyalty has drawn most of its illustrations from the national level. But what has been said of national loyalty can also be said of those loyalties that transcend nations or operate at lower levels within them. People can feel special attachments to their sex, race, social class, regions or families. They can feel loyalty toward their schools, universities, regiments, political parties, international ideologies or religions. The ties that bind them can be positive ones of gratitude or of moral conviction. I may be loyal to my family or my school because I am grateful for what they have given me. Or I may be loyal to my region or my class because they need my support. Or I may be loyal to my political party or my religion because I believe that they represent certain important truths or values.

Yet here, too, the ties that bind can also be negative ones. I may be loyal to my family simply because they offer me some kind of defence against the world outside. I may be loyal to my school because it represents a childhood idyll into which I can retreat from the responsibilities and challenges of adulthood. I may be loyal to my region or class or race out of resentment against others. Loyalty to one's own tribe (or tribes) at these trans- or sub-national levels is just as vulnerable to corruption, and by the same psychic forces, as its national equivalent.

The kinds of corruption we have considered thus far have all vitiated attitudes toward outsiders. But there is another kind that poisons regard for certain insiders; namely, the urge to find a scapegoat. A scapegoat is someone or some group that is made to bear the guilt of their own community. It is essential that it be possible to regard the scapegoat as belonging to this community, for otherwise the transference of guilt would not be plausible. The government could not easily blame the opposition for a failure of its own policy; but it could plausibly concentrate responsibility upon a particular minister. The process of scapegoating involves the transference of blame from the community as a whole onto the shoulders of one of its parts. The scapegoat is the Enemy Within.

The urge to find a scapegoat may be nothing more than the common desire to pass the buck. But it may equally be driven by the need to get some kind of grasp on a persistently bewildering problem, to isolate its cause and deal with it. Human beings do not rest easily without answers; and when the problem is sufficiently worrisome, we will often prefer a fabricated answer to none at all.

One common form of scapegoating is racism. When one is looking for someone or some body to blame, suspicion naturally falls on those who are different, and whose differences unnerve or threaten or annoy. For example, in times when people are bewildered by economic distress – by rampant inflation that is wiping out their life's savings, or by widespread unemployment that is stripping them of their livelihood, their social function, and much of their *raison d'être* – and when the causes of this distress are impersonal and mysterious, it is quite understandable that they should be strongly driven to make some sense out of their predicament, establish some kind of control, by identifying who is responsible. And the stranger in their midst presents an easy target. Hence the growth of anti-semitism in Weimar Germany in the 1920s and 1930s; or of contemporary racism in Britain's inner cities.

But scapegoats are not chosen simply because they are different. They may be chosen also because of some long-standing prejudice; or because they appear to be profiting from the present distress; or because they seem to flout indigenous custom; or because their behaviour is, in fact, offensive. It does not encourage feelings of affection and generosity, for example, to greet someone by offering the hand of friendship, only to find it hanging there unmet because he, a hasidic Jew, regards you, a Gentile, as unclean. And it severely strains tolerance to stand

in a stationary and lengthening queue outside a public tele-
phone box (the old, red, closed kind), while an Asian woman
inside conducts a leisurely conversation, blithely ignoring the
irritated tapping on the windows, and then, when deciding to
exit, does not so much as offer a word of apology (because she
cannot speak English).

Sometimes hostility towards strangers is not entirely born
of the insecurity and malice of the indigenous community.
Sometimes strangers are not entirely blameless of helping to
kindle the resentment that they suffer. Certainly, natives have a
duty to recognize the vulnerability of immigrants, and to be
hospitable toward them. But equally immigrants have a duty to
learn and respect the customs of those among whom they have
come to dwell.

Still, this is not to condone racism. To recognize that racial
prejudice sometimes has some of its roots in the insensitive
behaviour of strangers, is not at all to say that the abuse they
subsequently suffer is largely their own fault. Racism, like any
form of hatred, is not by nature discriminate in its judgements.
It is not naturally careful to be fair. Its victims invariably get
blamed for all manner of wickedness. Their character is thickly
painted in a single shade of deepest black. What is more, the
individual is reduced to a type, identified simply as a chip off
the collective block. The apparent goodwill of this individual is
entirely eclipsed by the certain malevolence of their tribe.
Whatever guilt Whites or Blacks, Jews or Gentiles are supposed
to bear, *this* White or *this* Black or *this* Jew or *this* Gentile is
assumed to bear too. In the eyes of racists there are no individuals, only specimens.

The racist corruption of tribal loyalty, like other kinds,
thrives on unjust generalizations, on the indiscriminate denigration of others. Such lying serves the purpose of eclipsing
the unflattering side of the truth about oneself. It makes it
possible to locate the roots of the problem at hand entirely
*else*where. It excuses one from responsibility. But the virulent
zeal with which the chosen Enemy is demonized betrays an
uneasy conscience. Reflecting on his experience in the former
Yugoslavia, Michael Ignatieff has written of national tribalism
that it

81

is a form of speech which shouts, not merely so that it will be heard, but so that it will believe itself. It was almost as if the quotient of crude historical fiction, violent moral exaggeration, ludicrous caricature of the enemy was in direct proportion to the degree to which the speaker was himself aware that it was all really a pack of lies ... That such fantasies do take hold of large numbers of people is a testament to the deep longing such people have to escape the stubborn realities of life.[11]

But what good did the flight into poisonous fantasy ever achieve? The denial of one's own share of responsibility makes it impossible to begin unpicking the real problem. And the wholesale shifting of blame onto others only multiplies the stock of injury and grievance.

A first step toward drawing the poison out of tribal affection, then, is to embark upon the practice of telling the truth. The whole truth. Not only about how They have wounded Us, but also about what We did to provoke Them. Not only about the noble deeds of our ancestors, but also about their cruel deeds and their callous omissions. Truth-telling involves the making of confession, the readiness to suffer the pain and depression of owning fault, and the humiliation of waiting upon another's forgiveness. But all this for the sake of peace, both within the soul and on the streets.

A further step in the process of detoxification is to make one's tribe as much a subject to justice as a champion of it. A tribe to be proud of is one that lives by the justice it demands. One that can respect foreigners, recognize their superior qualities or their peculiar virtues, and be willing to learn from them. One that can take responsibility for injuries committed in its name. A tribe to be proud of is one that can do these things and feel, not diminished, but stronger. One that knows that it does not have to be perfect or dominant in order to be worthwhile. One that can celebrate the unique grace of its own manners and customs, the unique grasp of reality that its language affords, the unique form that justice takes in its institutions – and *still* confess its shortcomings and acknowledge the virtues of others. One that measures its own health more by its readiness to grow in wisdom and virtue, than by self-satisfaction in the perfection of its achievements.

Loyalty to one's tribe, then, should not consist in denying its faults and scapegoating or denigrating others. That performs no good service. Genuine loyalty is prophetic. It cares for the tribe's integrity more than for its dominance or its comfort. It holds its own people accountable to the ideals with which they identify themselves, denouncing them when they betray their calling, and urging them to be true to it. Paradoxically, then, the epitome of true loyalty is to stand on the side of foreigners whom one's own people have wronged. This is the loyalty that Yevgeni Yevtushenko declares in 'Babii Yar', his poem about Russian anti-semitism:

> Oh my Russian people!
> I know you are internationalists to the core.
> But those with unclean hands
> have often made a jingle of your purest name.
> I know the goodness of my land . . .
>
> In my blood there is no Jewish blood.
> In their callous rage all anti-semites
> must hate me now as a Jew.
> For that reason I am a true Russian![12]

Those who are truly loyal to their tribe are those who would make it loyal to humanity.

7

TOLERANCE
. . . NOT INDIFFERENCE

Error has no rights. That is the gist of what Pope Pius XII once said in some comments on toleration.[1] Error has no rights at least because it is dangerous and at most because it is wilful. Whether or not it results from a deliberate choice to obscure the truth, erroneous belief issues in wrong behaviour, and wrong behaviour harms both the agent and his neighbours, in body or in soul. Because it is harmful, and sometimes deliberate, error should not be tolerated.

The Pope, of course, had particular kinds of error in mind. He was not thinking of arithmetic inaccuracy. Or of oversights in scientific experiments. Or of own goals on the football pitch. What he had in mind was religious and moral error of a fundamental kind, whether in belief or in practice. Arguably, as kinds of mistakes go, these are among the more serious.

Nevertheless, they do not seem to worry us to the same extent that they worried him. We do not seem to regard unorthodox belief or practice as a threat to the social and political order, far less as a threat to the soul. Indeed, we are loathe to call unorthodoxy 'error' at all. For us, the toleration of contrary thoughts and ways is a strength not a weakness, a virtue not a vice.

Why?

One reason lies in the European experience of a hundred years or so of intermittent strife between Catholics and Protestants from about 1550 to about 1650 – strife that blew up into civil war in France and into an international war that caused what is now Germany to lose one-third of its population.

Before that experience it was more easily assumed that (true) religion is a force for social cohesion, since it provides the ultimate ground of all moral order and the deepest source of all moral obligation. Certainly, medieval Christendom had long been aware of rival claimants to the status of the one true religion, but it had succeeded either in excluding their adherents from the mainstream of social life (the Jews) or in keeping them outside its walls altogether (the Muslims). Besides, these rivals were so different as to be easily dismissed as infidels. Neither Judaism nor Islam, therefore, posed any threat to the internal cohesion of Christian civilization and of Christian societies. But the emergence of Protestantism did. For here was a movement *within* the one true religion contending for an alternative understanding of its nature; and unlike earlier heretics, Protestants could not be suppressed by force of arms. So, in the aftermath of the Wars of Religion, some political thinkers in Europe began the liberal search for conditions of political unity and social harmony that expressly do not depend on contentious religious belief. Thomas Hobbes, for example, located the basis of political community, not in the revealed law of God, but in the enlightened self-interest of each individual.[2]

Because of the traumatic experience of the Wars of Religion, then, religion came to be seen by many, not as a pillar of society, but rather as a threat. It became associated with an uncompromising dogmatism, willing to shed blood in order to secure the hegemony of a partisan (and questionable) vision of the truth. In contrast to this, the virtuousness of tolerance appeared stark.

The threat posed by religion to social peace is one reason why we value tolerance. Another reason, already touched upon in Chapters One and Three, is that we have become much more openly sceptical about religious truth. Or, at least, we no longer defer to traditional religious authorities. We do not trust their competence to distinguish truth from error in these matters. Indeed, we hardly trust anyone's competence other than our own: religious belief has become a matter of entirely 'private' truth. This is partly because such belief has become embarrassing. It has become embarrassing because the ascendancy in modern times of a covert combination of natural science and materialist metaphysics has made it seem implausible.[3] And even though that ascendancy is now waning, and it is becoming clearer that the 'scientific' method gives natural science no legitimate authority to pronounce upon the existence or non-existence of non-material realities, the implausibility of religious belief is still widely assumed.

Ironically, this assumption persists in spite of widespread religious experience. As mentioned in Chapter Two, social scientific research in Great Britain (and the United States) has revealed that about 70 per cent of adults claim to have had a significant 'religious' experience.[4] But it has also revealed that many of these adults are ashamed to speak of their experiences, because they fear ridicule.[5] What this suggests is that religious belief lacks, not so much empirical grounding, as public esteem and a publicly approved language to give it voice. And until it gains such esteem and such language from the leaders of public opinion, it will be an embarrassment. And so long as it remains an embarrassment, it will be kept private. It will be kept private because it is considered insecure and incapable of surviving in the hostile world of public criticism. But this strategic withdrawal from public scrutiny quickly gives rise to the opinion that religious belief is properly a purely private matter, that it makes no claims to be true, that no one has the right to judge what I happen to prefer to believe. Religious belief, then, becomes virtually an aesthetic preference, about which others may say, 'It's not to my taste', but not, 'It's wrong.' In other words, it deserves tolerance in the sense of a suspension of judgement.

A third reason why tolerance sits so high on our list of values is that we have come to celebrate individuality and difference. Others may find these threatening and unsettling, but we find them stimulating and exciting. They can add colour and variety and spice to social life. They can enrich it. What is more, in those spheres of life where we still believe in the possibility of knowing the truth, the appearance of something different and unfamiliar can actually advance our knowledge. It can move us to question our assumptions. It can alert us to features or facets of reality that we have not noticed before.

The marketplace of ideas should be free, then, so that our stock of knowledge and understanding might be refined and increased. We must tolerate what first appears to us to be non-sense because, upon further consideration, it might turn out to have something to teach us.

A final reason for our valuing tolerance is that the free market of ideas is a bulwark against political totalitarianism. Tolerance permits the circulation of ideas that may not suit the powers-that-be. It permits the telling of stories in versions that are not officially approved. In other words, it nourishes criticism of those who rule, their institutions and their policies. This is, in part, why liberal societies are very reluctant to permit censorship, lest those who wield political power use it to silence voices that tell inconvenient truths or present alternative points of view.

These, then, are some of the reasons we value tolerance so highly and regard it as a virtue. But there is a measure of ambiguity about what exactly tolerance is. For although it is certainly a letting-be of opinions or practices with which one disagrees, there are different ways of letting-be.

On the one hand, one can let something be *and* let it alone. In other words, one can let it be by giving it space to exist and then keeping it at a safe arm's length. I can hear you out, recognize that what you say is not what I would say, and then pronounce blandly, 'Well, that's different!', before changing the subject. This is the lazy, perhaps even cowardly, tolerance that is born of indifference. I let what is contrary exist, but I allow it no power to affect me. I go through the motions of paying it respect, but I don't really take it seriously. I don't engage with it. I'm not prepared to put myself at such risk.

This kind of tolerance is actually demeaning. It is the patronizing kind that, according to A. J. Ayer, British colonial administrators in Africa used to show toward the natives – 'the tolerance of the schoolmaster, displayed toward his boys so long as they behaved themselves'.[6] And it is often felt as an injury by those who receive it. That is why 'the tolerated are increasingly demanding to be appreciated, not ignored, and becoming more sensitive to suggestions of contempt lurking beneath the condescension. They do not want to be told that differences do not matter, that they can think what they like, provided they keep to themselves . . .'[7]

But tolerance need not patronize. For it is possible that I might be prepared *both* to let something exist *and* pay close attention to what it is and what it says. To recognize and acknowledge, not only where it differs from my ways and thoughts, but also where it contradicts and challenges them. And not only to acknowledge, but to consider and assess, and then to answer. If this were the manner of my letting be, then I would be displaying the tolerance born of care, not of demeaning indifference.

But care for what? Certainly, care for the other person. Care in the sense of respect for their freedom to think and believe as they do. But more than this. Also care to understand exactly what it is that they believe. Care to understand what they mean by what they believe. For example, someone may say to me, 'I don't believe in God.' If I care enough to take this seriously, I will not leave the matter there but will respond by asking, 'OK, but which God don't you believe in?' Suppose they answer, 'I don't believe in the Christian God.' Then, in order to understand what they mean by their unbelief, I must enquire further: 'What do you understand the Christian God to be? And why don't you believe in him? Is it because you've worked your way through all the philosophical arguments for the existence of an almighty and benevolent Creator, and concluded that none of them add up? Or is it because your own experience of Christians has been off-putting? Or because you've inherited certain prejudices from your parents that you've never thought to challenge? Or because you're a Muslim, and that therefore Christianity is inextricably bound up in your mind with the humiliations and abuses meted out upon the Islamic world in modern times by the west? Or is it because you've a hunch that committing yourself to belief in such a God would involve inconvenient changes to your life?' And so on. The point here is that a tolerance that cares, cares enough to take the trouble to find out what is meant by what is said. And since our deeper beliefs about the nature and meaning of things invariably bear the marks of our particular lives, someone who wants to understand what we believe must take the time, and have the patience and sensitivity, to get to know us well.

But such carefulness with what is said implies something even more. It implies a care for truth. If we lack care for truth – perhaps because we doubt that it can be known – why should we bother to get to grips with beliefs that on first appearance we don't like or don't agree with?[8] The only ultimately satisfactory rationale for taking pains to understand what another person says, is that we care to find out the truth by ascertaining whether what is said agrees with what we ourselves already believe; or whether it disagrees, is wrong and can be discounted; or whether it disagrees, is right and needs to be taken on board. The tolerance that cares respects contrary opinion as a possible bearer of truth. That is why it troubles to pay searching attention.

This kind of tolerance, then, engages with what it lets be. It engages it in dialogue. And the conduct of genuine dialogue certainly requires much more than the regulation tilt of the head, gaze of the eyes and sympathetic purring. It requires, first and foremost, a care for truth; but then also patience, self-restraint, generosity, candour, a willingness to be taught, honesty and courage. As one contemporary exponent of the principles of dialogue puts it:

> All participants must respect one another as persons responsible to the truth and bound to act in accord with conscience . . . Each should assume that all have something to contribute, that all can benefit from what others have to give, and that all must judge for themselves what they can accept from others. Participants should presume that another's communication is well-intentioned, and each should try to grasp the elements of others' communications in their total personal context, that is, in the light of the factors which actually determine and limit their meaning. Each party should declare honestly and without compromise what he or she thinks true, while expecting and encouraging others to do the same; there should be no excessive eagerness to eliminate differences, since these must not be suppressed but transcended by means which respect responsibility to

truth and personal freedom. Participants in dialogue should treat differences and oppositions as important, and deal with them patiently.[9]

A tolerance that genuinely respects what differs from it and even opposes it, will care to engage it in dialogue. It will not just let it be alone and in silence. Rather, it will let it be while addressing it. True tolerance, then, is not the same as a careless indifference to what others think and do, so long as they do not get in the way. It does not treat the other person as an atomistic individual whose ways and thoughts have no necessary bearing on one's own. On the contrary, while respecting the freedom of others to be different, it seeks to communicate with them, to identify points of agreement and points of disagreement, and to strive to reduce the latter. It invites others to co-operate in a common search for truth and, by fostering the growth of co-operative virtues, it creates community.

But the ability of tolerance to do this is limited by the willingness of both parties to engage in dialogue. And sometimes they are not willing. What, then, should tolerance do? What can it do when faced with the religious fundamentalist, the moral dogmatist or the political ideologue? It cannot build community (yet). But it can care to suppress angry, frustrated reactions in itself. It can exercise the care of patience with regard to the other. It can care to resist the desire to turn its back on him and storm out the door. It can care to strain to see beyond the other's words in the hope of discerning the fears and hurts that make him so wooden-headed and unbending. And then, perhaps, seeing what he means through what he says, it might be able to address the powerful emotions that underlie and rigidify his thinking, soothe them, and gently coax him into the co-operative work of dialogue.

But sometimes the fundamentalist is not just unbending but abusive. And sometimes the political ideologue is not just strident but violent. Would tolerance stand aside and let abuse and violence advance? Those whose tolerance is born of indifference might well, so long as they reckon that they themselves are not going to suffer. But those who are tolerant because they care would not, because they care about the truth, above all the truth about what human well-being is and what serves it and what destroys it. Such people are prepared to give the benefit of the doubt to what seems at first sight to be erroneous, until it becomes patently clear that such error really is harmful to human goods and could be curtailed at reasonable cost.

'But who is to say what the human goods are,' someone might protest, 'and who is to say what is harmful to them? And according to whose opinions, then, should the line be drawn beyond which tolerance may not extend itself?'

Let it be granted that these are sometimes controversial matters; nevertheless, all societies, including liberal ones, draw the line somewhere. Even liberal societies and institutions outlaw physical violence, except in cases where it is necessary to fend off criminal injury. As one apologist for liberalism has written: 'Duelling was a voluntary exchange between consenting adults; but liberals never hesitated, in this case, to enforce state prohibitions against individual choice.'[10] Many liberal societies also outlaw anything that can be construed as an incitement to racial hatred. And some even outlaw behaviour that can be perceived as demeaning to women or minorities. Every society regards some kinds of conduct as intolerable, and liberal societies are characteristically keen to defend certain goods by maintaining rights against injury. There are always some things that should not be put up with, and need to be actively countered by law and, if need be, by authorized force. Tolerance always has its limits.

The difference, then, between our liberal society and more authoritarian ones, whether in our own past or in someone else's present, is not that they have an orthodoxy to defend and we do not. It is not simply that we are *laissez-faire* with regard to ideas and conduct and they are not. The difference is merely that our orthodoxy differs from theirs and that we are more *laissez-faire* than they. We have prevalent notions of what is good and valuable, as they do. We have notions of what is harmful, as they do. We take steps to protect what is valuable against harm, as they do. For reasons given above, we value freedom of speech and of religious and sexual practice more than authoritarian societies. We do not necessarily regard such freedom as morally unambiguous. We may well recognize that it permits people to do harm to themselves and others. But we may nevertheless judge it worthwhile to allow such harm, for the sake of preventing worse evils and of enabling the realization of certain goods. For example, we may consider it worthwhile to permit the exhibition of (arguably) pornographic 'art' as the necessary price of having a (relatively) free market of ideas, and because the cost of suppressing them would be the concession of too much power to the state. And we may have very certain convictions that some kinds of sexual behaviour are psychologically and socially harmful, and yet still hold with Pierre Trudeau, Prime Minister of Canada in the 1960s, that 'the state has no place in the bedrooms of the nation'. If we are more *laissez-faire* than other societies, that is because we disagree with them over what is harmful and over the price we are prepared to pay for curtailing harm. It is not because we do not recognize any behaviour as harmful and therefore tolerate everything. Not at all. There are some moral errors to which even we liberals deny rights.

The reason for labouring this point is to show that, although liberal societies have appeared, through the relaxation of the law, to assume a position of moral neutrality with regard to certain kinds of behaviour previously outlawed – most obviously forms of sexual behaviour such as adultery and homosexual practice – there are nevertheless many other matters on which they are very much morally committed. Indeed, liberal tolerance in its fullest and most adequate form rests on definite moral convictions – for example, about the value of knowing the truth, and about the dialogical virtues required to discover it. It is highly important, therefore, that liberals have the courage and the consistency to own these convictions and contend for their rational grounds – even if that compels them to espouse metaphysical realities. Because, if they do not, the tolerance born of care will easily be overwhelmed by the unchecked tide of moral nihilism. Then the only tolerance left standing will be that which serves to free individuals to pursue their own private goals, undistracted by the claims of responsibility. And, come the day when a contrary opinion or practice stands in the way of that pursuit, let there be no doubt that the pseudo-tolerance of private convenience will reveal itself in all its natural ruthlessness.

8

COMMUNITY
. . . HOW CAN WE BUILD IT?

There is in the air a sense that something is awry with British society. Intermittently, in books and newspapers, on TV and radio, in pubs and Parliament, from government ministers and opposition spokesmen, from pulpits and in the streets, we hear murmurings of such things as 'moral anarchy' and 'social disintegration'. Apocalyptic statistics are invoked, showing the apparently relentless rise in crime and divorce. Chilling stories are retold of acts of arbitrary and gruesome violence wrought by those we had assumed were too young to be so corrupt: the battering to death in Liverpool of a young child by two eleven-year-olds; and the throat-cutting of a taxi-driver in London by an eighteen-year-old public schoolboy who had been 'dared' by a friend to murder a complete stranger. And then, of course, mention is made of the seeming pandemic of sexual abuse of children by adults, often parents.

THE ROOTS OF COMMUNITY IN FRIENDSHIP

These are some of the alleged symptoms. But what is supposed to be the malaise?

As one influential diagnosis would have it, the disease from which we suffer is the decline among us of a sense of community.[1] What is meant by 'sense of community' is not always clear. But one obvious meaning is the sense of being a member of a social whole, belonging to it, identifying with it, feeling responsible for it. This involves regarding society as more than just a means by which individuals can pursue their purely private ends more efficiently. It involves thinking of it as bound together by more than just a set of expedient 'social contracts' in which a number of essentially isolated individuals agree to surrender certain liberties, in order to secure some otherwise unobtainable private advantages – for example, a higher degree of security from injury at their neighbours' hands. To have a sense of being a member of a community involves regarding membership as, in some sense, valuable in itself, and not just as an instrument for some other purpose.

'In some sense'?

Take friendship as a kind of community. It may well be that those who are party to a friendship gain certain private benefits from it. Someone may receive from a friend help in preparing for exams, or a loan with which to pacify the bank manager, or an invitation to visit the family château. But the value of friendship in this case – if it *is* genuine friendship – is *more* than its value as a means of obtaining these and other such benefits. Friendship has a value in itself. It is an intrinsic, and not just an instrumental, good. The good of friendship displays itself in such things as conversation, where the point is as much to journey together as to arrive at any particular destination. This good is realized in acts of sheer care; where, for example, one friend asks questions of another out of serious curiosity – about who he or she is and what makes them tick – and the other grants answers. The former seeks simply the privilege of being entrusted with knowledge of their friend; the latter is delighted simply to give the gift of such knowledge. The point of this exercise is essentially internal to it: to know and to be known, to trust and to be trusted, to love and to be loved. Simply.

It is perfectly true, of course, that friends 'get something out' of friendship; but what they get out of it is, basically, friendship itself. Perhaps it would be better to say that friends get something *within* friendship; which means that they get something in the very process of giving and of caring for what is given.

Friendship, then, is a reality in which individuals participate. In order for it to exist, individuals have to invest themselves in it; they have to give themselves to each other. They remain individuals, but not isolated atoms. They are personally connected.

They are individuals-in-community, members of a larger whole. If the whole flourishes, they will flourish with it. And if the whole fails, they will suffer with it – and bear the psychic marks of its demise for the rest of their lives.

To be a friend is to be personally invested in the larger, social reality of friendship. And this is made up of individuals *and* the relations that not merely connect them (as it were, externally), but involve them.

Obviously, friendship is a kind of community, but to what extent can we take it as representative of community as such? In what sense can we describe as 'friends' members of a family, a neighbourhood, a school, a church, a club, a business, a charitable organization, or a citizenry? Except in the case of a family, such members often have very little in the way of personal investment in each other. They may know very little about each other outside their particular social role, and they may have little interest in acquiring such knowledge. Their relationships with each other may be considerably instrumental. Indeed, the fact that they are related at all may simply be the result of their being engaged in a common enterprise. Fellow-members, of course, may become intimate friends; but being intimate friends is not the same as being fellow-members.

At first glance, then, it might seem that friendship cannot be taken as basic to all forms of community. Either that, or we must start to redescribe neighbourhoods, schools and so forth as, at best, quasi-communities. But to do this would be to concede too quickly that the cohesion and flourishing of such social bodies owes nothing to the 'friendly' quality of personal relationships. Certainly, it is conceivable that members of a business, whether governmental, commercial, or charitable, might relate to one another simply as social functionaries. Managers might regard their subordinates simply in terms of their role in the organization. 'After all,' they might say, 'we're not here to pass the time of day in exchanging social pleasantries. We're here to produce goods efficiently and to keep this business afloat!' But if managers were to take this attitude, and if such an example were to set the tone for the rest of the bodies of which they had charge, then they would end up with resentful and unco-operative (and therefore less than optimally efficient) workforces. For no one enjoys being treated merely as a function or an instrument. Everyone wants their dignity as a person to be acknowledged and respected. And this involves more than just not being made the object of abuse. It also involves more than being treated with fairness. It involves being offered a measure of sympathy and care – a measure of kindness or friendliness, in which we are met as equals.

It is now virtually a commonplace of management theory that the success of a business (or any organization) depends partly on its 'culture' or ethos. That is to say, it depends on the extent to which it inspires a sense of community among its members. In part, this principle of economic efficiency rests on the recognition that people are more highly motivated to work for an enterprise that they can regard as, in some sense, their own. In order to foster this sense of identification, several strategies are now commonly recommended. One is to give all employees some kind of financial stake in the company – whether through shareholding or through a scheme that links pay-bonuses to profits. Another is to give employees some measure of participation in the making of decisions that will affect the nature, the conditions, or, indeed, the very possibility of their work. A third is to devolve power and responsibility to smaller units.

These last two strategies are not designed just to foster the employees' sense of belonging. They also aim to make the business more efficient in its delivery of goods by enabling it to learn from the experience of its members, and by enabling it to respond to changing local conditions more sensitively and rapidly. According to one management guru, Peter Senge, a successful business should take the form, not of a hierarchy, but of a federation of 'teams'. The ethos of these teams should be essentially egalitarian, with members complementing each other's strengths and compensating for each other's weaknesses. Communication should be in the form of dialogue, rather than the issuing and obeying of commands; for in this way the team will be able to learn quickly, and adjust and improve its performance accordingly.[2] Significantly, Senge recognizes that the practice of dialogue both requires and fosters friendship – a willingness to abandon the pursuit of power as such, to lay aside status as a political weapon, to be self-critical, to be vulnerable in the admission of ignorance and the confession of fault, to be forgiving of mistakes, and to trust others to do likewise.[3]

Not all the strategies for fostering a sense of community within a business are concerned with the reform of organizational structures. Another, more recent one, seeks to promote a 'shared vision', often by means of the formulation and publication of a 'mission statement' that expresses the values and aims of the enterprise. Sometimes, the rationale given for this is merely that corporate cohesion and dynamism are strengthened when individual members are committed to *a* common set of aims or principles or guiding practices. The claim here is merely formal: the vital, substantive question of *which* set of aims, and so forth, members should adopt, is not broached. Senge is a little bolder and allows himself to slide from talking about a shared vision of 'what we want to create', to 'what we deeply care about accomplishing', to 'ultimate intrinsic desires', to (at last) 'goals of intrinsic value'.[4] He recognizes that it is not enough for a business's mission to be 'common'; it must also be 'ennobling', holding out the prospect of adding value to the world.[5] Implicitly, therefore, he recognizes that employees are moral beings as well as economic and rational ones; and that it is therefore important to them, not only to promote their financial interests or to have an appropriate measure of the power of self-determination, but also (and perhaps above all) to invest themselves in activity that is structured by genuinely moral purposes.

All this sounds good. But is it sincere? That is, do managers really see their employees in all of their human dimensions, or are they just going through the motions for the sake of economic efficiency? Do they really respect those who work for them, or are they just manipulating them? If they are not sincere, then that is bound to become apparent in their behaviour. Are they too busy to look their employees in the eye as they pass by, and greet them? Do they ever stop to chat? Do they remember them by name? Do they always find subtle ways of reminding them who's boss, and putting them in their place? Do they really listen to what employees tell them? Do they take the time to make adequate responses? Do they take the trouble to listen again? Do they ever act on what employees tell them? Insincerity is hard to disguise for long; and when it is exposed, it will only serve to intensify resentment among the workforce. For if employees dislike being used, they dislike being deceived even more. So for a business to become a healthy and co-operative community, it is not enough that its managers should modify forms of remuneration, increase formal opportunities for participation in decision-making, or formulate a business creed. In addition, managers need to shape themselves. They need to cultivate virtues in themselves – for example, the readiness to let their own behaviour be defined by what they owe other people; the modesty to recognize that, though leaders of a body of people have the greater share of power and responsibility (and sometimes the greater share of talent), the led are equally essential to the efficient operation of the whole; the patience to listen hard; the honesty to recognize good advice; the humility to take it from humble quarters; and the generosity to give it due credit.[6]

Even in the case of a business, then, it is arguable that friendship or, at least, friendliness between fellow members, and especially between managers and their subordinates, is important for corporate flourishing.

What is true of a business is true, *a fortiori*, of a family, a school or a church, where friendship or education in friendly dealings with other people is (or should be) a large part of these institutions' *raison d'être*. It is also true, *a fortiori*, of a club, which is specifically designed to bring together people of like mind, experience or interest, with a view to fostering friendship; and of a neighbourhood, which flourishes only in so far as its members behave toward one another as (friendly) neighbours.

But what of a citizenry? Is it possible to regard this as a social body that requires a measure of friendship to flourish?

Aristotle would have answered, Yes. But then he was talking about the citizenry of small Greek city-states, where the majority of members were slaves, not citizens; and the aristocratic minority of citizens, being free from the demands of manual labour, had the leisure to cultivate close personal relations with their fellows. In contrast, the citizenry of modern democratic nation-states often number tens, if not hundreds, of millions of people, the vast majority of whom are totally unknown to each other. What form could friendship possibly take here? Or does a citizenry not comprise a community as we have defined it?

Since most citizens are entirely unknown to each other, it would seem that they cannot meaningfully be called friends. Yet in so far as citizens expect, when encountering a stranger, to be met not just with indifference but with care, and with a care that is at least respectful though preferably kind, we can say that when citizens do come across each other they expect to be treated (and presumably to treat) with friendliness. E. M. Forster dramatizes this point in *A Passage to India*. The Indian Dr Aziz, charged with rape, is acquitted because his English complainant, Miss Quested, withdraws her accusation. But Aziz is not satisfied: '[for] while relieving the oriental mind she had chilled it, with the result that he could scarcely believe that she was sincere, and indeed from his standpoint she was not. For her behaviour rested on cold justice and honesty; she had felt, while she recanted, no passion of love for those whom she had wronged. Truth is not truth in that exacting land unless there go with it kindness . . .'[7] Not in India. Nor elsewhere.

Now, of course, many of us have ceased to expect friendly treatment from strangers, living as we do in fast-paced urban locations where people do not have (or make) the time to be courteous, to acknowledge, to smile, to greet, to chat, to pass (a little of) the time of day. But the truth is that our expectations have not simply ceased; they have been disappointed. Had they simply ceased, we would not be moved to remark upon the carelessness, if not the aggressiveness, we experience from other people as we walk down the street. We certainly would not remark upon it in the tones of indignation that we do. We may not expect strangers to be friendly any more, but when they are not we still complain. We complain because we feel injured; for although we have ceased to expect friendliness, we nevertheless feel that we deserve it. And when we find ourselves in a place where the natives are spontaneously friendly, how delighted we are.

Citizens are not fully-fledged friends, but they do participate in a weak form of friendship. They do not know and love each other intimately. But they do feel that they owe their fellow citizens, and are owed by them, a measure of care.

If the direct relationship between citizens is often only a weak form of friendship, their indirect relationship through their political representatives can be a much stronger form. For whereas it is impossible for tens of millions or so of British voters, for example, to enjoy friendship with one another except in an extenuated sense, it is not impossible for their several hundred MPs.

Indeed, friendship is extremely important for the quality of parliamentary life, because it is a vital ingredient of fruitful political debate. If political debate is to be fruitful, it has to be more than the mutual exchange of opposing political dogmas. It has to be more than an exercise in political point-scoring, carried out for the entertainment of TV audiences. It has to be more than a ritualized extension of warfare. It has to be a dialogue. Therefore, it requires a measure of friendship.

For, as we have argued in Chapter Seven, genuine dialogue has the nature of a common enterprise, whose participants share the aim of discovering the truth and use each other to test their perceptions of it. If this enterprise is to succeed, then those involved need to be frank about what they do not know or are not sure about. They need to resist the temptation to hide from view the weaknesses in their own arguments. They need to eschew manipulative tactics, such as making a (subtle) personal attack or changing the subject in order to distract attention from the weakness of their own position, or making displays of cleverness in order to intimidate, or pulling rank in order to suppress. They also need to be quick to give credit where credit is due; and to adopt whoever's opinions seem more reasonable and cogent. For the point of dialogue is not for one party to win by demonstrating her superiority over the other, but for all the parties to discover the truth together. Successful dialogue, therefore, requires the exercise of co-operative, friendly virtues such as honesty, trust, vulnerability, and generosity. But more than this, it requires an interest in understanding why others hold views that differ from one's own. Why do they begin from different premises? What has led them to choose this starting-point and not that one? Often the answers to such questions will be rooted in the biography of the person addressed. Their final appeal will be to some insight or conviction born of a particular experience. So, in order to gain deep understanding of a contrary opinion, we must ultimately take an interest in the one who holds it; and, if our curiosity is to be satisfied, then we must earn the right to be granted a measure of intimacy. And that will require the demonstration of respect, patience and care. In sum, successful dialogue involves the nurturing of a degree of friendship.

Could it be that current disillusionment with politics in the western world, which is indicated by low public regard for the integrity of politicians and the large and increasing numbers of voters who choose not to vote at elections, has something to do with a failure to let the requirements of friendship govern the manner of public debate?[8] When did you ever hear a politician say, in answer to a question, 'I don't know'? And how often do you hear members of one political party publicly approving of a policy or a decision made by members of another? In domestic and professional life, someone who refuses to admit their ignorance when it is patent to everyone around, is regarded with contempt. Likewise, someone who refuses ever to give credit to an opponent, from whom it is perfectly obvious that they have borrowed ideas. Is it any surprise, then, when politicians so often reduce public debate to the level of a childish squabble, in which no one has the maturity to concede anything to anyone, that they lose respect, and politics loses its dignity, in the eyes of the public?

SYMPTOMS OF DECLINE

My argument is that friendship is basic to all forms of community, and that the sense of being a member of a community is akin to the sense of being involved in friendship: a sense of being personally invested in a relationship or set of relationships in which the parties are bound together by trust of and care for one another. According to communitarians, it is the decline of this sense that lies at the heart of our current social malaise.

But is this diagnosis true? Two kinds of evidence are commonly brought forward to support it: crime statistics on the one hand, and marriage and divorce statistics on the other.

Let's begin with crime. How accurate is the quite widespread perception that society is in the process of being engulfed in a rising tide of theft and violence? Tales of horrific murders put colour in the cheeks of this nightmare, but provide no sure basis in reality for it. Children and adolescents did not kill people for the first time in the 1990s, and they do not make a habit of doing so now. Serial killers are not the invention of the late-twentieth century. Remember Jack the Ripper?

If stories are unreliable indicators of general trends, statistics are often hard to interpret. In the case of crime statistics compiled by the police, for example, does a rise indicate an increase in crime or an increase in reportage? Less ambiguous than reports to the police, however, are statistics based on interviews with victims – such as those produced by the British Crime Survey (BCS). Taking this as our measure,[9] it is clear that the public's fear of crime exceeds the reality of it. According to a BBC poll,[10] people suppose that 26 per cent of the population have been the victim of violent crime in the past year; whereas, according to the BCS, the real figure is closer to 5 per cent.[11] This evidence of extreme exaggeration of the risks is corroborated by a recent police survey in Medway, an area of Kent that is moderately crime-ridden, and a nationwide National Opinion Poll (NOP) survey. In Medway public estimates of the murders in the area during the previous year ranged from 13 to 18, whereas the police had recorded only 1; and of burglaries from 17,000 to 20,000, whereas the BCS suggests a figure nearer 3,500.[12] The NOP survey in 1986 found that people on average guessed that 47 per cent of crime involves violence, whereas the BCS suggests 5 per cent.[13]

So, things may not be as bad as they seem. That is the good news. The bad news is that there is good reason to think that things have been getting worse, and getting worse fast. According to *both* official statistics *and* the BCS, crime in England and Wales rose rapidly between 1981 and 1993: by 111 per cent and 77 per cent, respectively.[14] During the period 1981–7, the BCS estimates an 80 per cent rise in bicycle theft, a 78 per cent rise in burglary attempts without loss, a 63 per cent rise in theft from a motor vehicle, a 39 per cent rise in burglary with loss, and a 36 per cent rise in theft of a motor vehicle.[15] And in the period 1988–92 it records a rise in assaults of almost 20 per cent, from 2.2m to 2.6m.[16]

It is true that total recorded crime in England and Wales fell by 5.5 per cent in 1993–4, and by 5 per cent in 1994–5; and that these decreases are not attributable to changes in recording practice, and should therefore be taken as real and not just apparent.[17] But it is far too early to claim that this signals a long-term trend: recorded crime also fell by 1 per cent in 1987–8 and 4 per cent in 1988–9, only to rise again by 13 per cent in 1989–90, 18 per cent in 1990–1, 11 per cent in 1991–2, and 4 per cent in 1992–3.[18]

There is good reason, then, to think that the number of crimes committed per annum has been rising rapidly in recent decades. That in itself is something to worry about. Another thing to worry about is that we *imagine* that the prevalence of criminal activity is much higher than it actually is. For our exaggerated fears themselves harm community. As *The Economist* puts it, 'fear of crime ... corrodes society almost as much as crime itself, isolating people in their homes and making them wary of contact with strangers'.[19] And it seems that our fear is growing. In 1984, 37 per cent of Britons polled said that they were afraid to answer their door at night. By 1992, the figure had risen to 54 per cent.[20]

So much for crime. What about marriage and divorce? According to a report published by the Joseph Rowntree Foundation, marriage rates in Britain have fallen to their lowest level since records began more than 150 years ago.[21] The number of people marrying each other has declined steadily for the past 20 years, from 17 per 1,000 members of the population to 11.[22] The number of people divorcing each other has increased six-fold since 1961.[23] According to one estimate, if the rate observed in 1987 were to continue, 37 per cent of British marriages solemnized would end in divorce.[24] Since then the rate has, in fact, increased from 12.7 to 13.7 per 1,000 married members of the population.[25]

The decline in the number of people marrying does not

necessarily indicate that all aspects of the institution of marriage are losing their appeal. A recent survey conducted by *The Independent* newspaper suggests that young people in Britain between the ages of 16 and 24 'yearn for long-term relationships, despite the evidence of divorce and separation all around them ... [and] still see traditional long-term relationships as their goal'.[26] Further, according to the Rowntree report, cohabitation tends to be a prelude rather than an alternative to marriage.[27] According to David Rose, assistant director of the British Household Panel Survey (BHPS), 'for a lot of young people cohabitation is replacing long engagement. But there is still a tremendous commitment to the family.'[28] And, in many cases where cohabitation is a permanent, rather than a provisional, substitute for marriage, couples make elaborate agreements and devices to demonstrate their commitment to each other and their children – for example, joint responsibility agreements, joint mortgages, and shared registering of children.[29]

Nevertheless, there is evidence that cohabitation is often associated with a weaker form of commitment than marriage. The BHPS concluded from its survey of 10,000 representative British people that 'cohabiting couples were more than four times as likely to split up as married couples'.[30] In 1992 the Office of Population Censuses and Surveys (OPCS) reported that 'of couples who married for the first time in the early 1980s, those who premaritally cohabited were 50 per cent more likely to have divorced after five years of marriage – and 60 per cent more likely to have divorced after eight years of marriage – than similar couples who had not premaritally cohabited'.[31] This should not be read as saying that the bond between cohabiting partners is necessarily weaker than that between a married couple. There are doubtless some instances of cohabitation where the mutual commitment is, in fact, stronger than in some instances of marriage. Still, the decision to cohabit rather than to marry is made in many cases precisely to avoid the irrevocability of the publicly declared vows of exclusive and permanent marital commitment. Often, then, it signifies a measure of initial hesitancy and reservation. Sometimes, the experience of living together confirms and strengthens mutual commitment, and the subsequent decision to marry is a sign of this. But there are other cases, all too frequent, where one cohabiting party – often the man — never enlarges his commitment, but is still induced by a sense of guilt into consenting to marry; and having done so, feels trapped and resentful. This, at least, is one plausible interpretation of the higher rate of divorce among couples who have cohabited before marriage.[32]

But why should divorce rates in general concern us? To some extent their rise is a result of what is arguably a healthy decline in our tolerance of abusive and exploitative behaviour within marriage. It is also the result of growing expectations of personal satisfaction within marriage, and a correlative unwillingness to put up with dissatisfaction.[33] What could be wrong with a couple deciding to end a relationship that they have both grown tired of, or that one partner never really wanted in the first place? Surely it's better for all concerned that they face up to the irredeemable misery of their marriage and make a clean break, rather than remain embroiled in marital warfare that damages them and their children (if they have any)?

Maybe.

The fact is, however, that divorce is never simply a 'clean break'. It may sometimes be preferable to the alternatives; but it is still damaging – to parents and children alike. Judging by statistics furnished by the OPCS, men and women at every age are more likely to die prematurely if they are divorced (or single or widowed) than if they are married.[34] Further, relative to their married counterparts, divorced men are twice as likely to die from heart disease;[35] divorced men and women are between four and six times as likely to be admitted to a mental hospital;[36] and divorced men are five times as likely – divorced women, three times – to attempt suicide.[37]

Of course, to observe a correlation between two phenomena is not yet to establish which of them is cause, and which of them effect. As *The Economist* has noted, 'some of the links may run both ways. For example, among both sexes, the divorced are the group most likely to be admitted to mental hospitals. This may simply prove that the unstable make difficult partners. Similarly, in Britain divorced men are the heaviest drinkers. But alcoholics may be less likely to marry and more likely to be thrown out by their partners than those who drink moderately.'[38] Fair point. Nevertheless, common sense surely tells us that the process of divorce is almost invariably a painful experience for the divorcing couple, and tends to leave them with deep wounds – feelings of worthlessness, inadequacy and guilt, together with a diminished capacity to trust themselves and others, and so to enter into relationships of intimacy. It is entirely reasonable, then, to expect divorce to have adverse effects on the physical, psychological and social health of the divorcees.

And also upon the health of their children.[39] In most cases, divorce entails for children considerably reduced contact with, and in many cases absolute loss of, one of their parents. In the US most divorced fathers ignore the offspring of their first marriages. According to the 1981 National Survey of Children, only 16 per cent of children saw their father as often as once a week on average; and almost half had not seen him at all in the twelve months preceding the survey. After ten years, only 10 per cent had weekly contact with their father and almost 66 per cent had not seen him in the past year.[40] In the UK, by the time divorce cases reach the courts, half of all children have lost touch with their father – and will probably never see him again.[41] Divorce means, then, that very many, if not most, children become members of single-parent families;[42] and, in general, this is not good news. To quote M. H. King and C. M. Elliot in the recent edition of the *Oxford Textbook of Medicine*:

> Individual children from single-parent families . . . do worse on average than those from traditional families in every dimension in which they are measured – physically, emotionally, behaviourally, educationally, economically, and in terms of smoking and drinking . . . They die earlier, do less well at school, are less well nourished, suffer more unemployment and are more prone to deviance and crime. They are between two and five times more susceptible to psychiatric illness, and run a higher risk of physical and psychological ill-health from the time of parental separation well into adult life. Even their bone age is delayed.[43]

This gloomy assessment is echoed by the distinguished sociologist, A. H. Halsey:

Such children, on the evidence available, tend to die earlier, to have more illness, to do less well at school, to exist at a lower level of nutrition, comfort and conviviality, to suffer more unemployment, to be more prone to deviance and crime, and finally to repeat the cycle of unstable parenting from which they have themselves been formed as relatively unsuccessful social personalities.[44]

There is, of course, heated debate about the causes of the disadvantages from which children in one-parent families tend to suffer. To some extent they can be attributed to the economic straits into which most single parents are plunged. A survey published by the Department of Social Security in 1991 suggested that of lone-parent families in Britain 60 per cent lacked any earnings, most relied heavily on social security benefits for their income, and 62 per cent described themselves as 'not very well off' or 'hard-pressed'.[45] The situation on the western side of the Atlantic is similar. An American study has found that separated and divorced women suffer an average fall of about 30 per cent in their income in the year after their marriage breaks up.[46] Nevertheless, poverty alone is not a sufficient explanation of the distress of children after divorce. The children of single parents register a higher average mortality rate than those in other low income groups;[47] and when their mother remarries, her children may no longer be poor, but they still continue to register the other ill-effects associated with divorce, sometimes even in stronger form.[48]

Again, common sense would say that divorce, especially when (as is often the case) it is acrimonious and results in the relative or absolute absence of the non-custodial parent, is bound to disturb (at least juvenile) children. It comes as no surprise, then, that a research project that followed a group of families for fifteen years found that

> three out of five children felt rejected by at least one of their parents after divorce, particularly where parents had remarried. Many blamed themselves. They saw themselves as straggling tail-ends of their parents' failed previous lives, as misfits, as mistakes. Their sense of identity was warped by feeling that the thing that had created them, the marriage

that brought them into being, had been rejected as failed and worthless. It left them uncertain of their own worth, and unwilling to trust others.[49]

It is important to note, however, that it is not so much divorce that causes the damage, as the manner of divorce.[50] There is evidence that children whose parents separate without acrimony and do not disappear from sight afterwards fare as well as children from stable families.[51] This suggests that, from the child's point of view, the separation of its parents from each other matters far less than the separation of either of them from it. It also suggests that some families where the marriage of the parents is intact, but where one or both parents have little to do with their children, might be more damaging than some families where the husband and wife are separated from each other but both continue to play parent. There is evidence that inadequate parental supervision and support, quite apart from divorce, sow trouble.[52] One American study has found that thirteen-year-old schoolchildren who take care of themselves for eleven or more hours a week are twice as likely to be abusers of marijuana, tobacco, or alcohol as those who were actively cared for by adults – regardless of socio-economic status.[53]

The notion that it is not so much divorce that is so disturbing for children as parental acrimony finds support elsewhere. Studies of the educational and behavioural deficits among children aged sixteen whose parents had divorced, have found that these deficits were present before the divorce occurred.[54] Further, some research reckons that criminal offending is twice as common among men raised in intact, two-parent homes where the parents are in conflict, as among those who grew up in one-parent families headed by an affectionate mother.[55] Finally, a survey of the results of ninety-two American and British studies concluded that the strongest effects of divorce on children are associated with parental conflict.[56]

But, in addition to parental absence and acrimony, there seems to be at least a third significant contributor to the distress of children after divorce: the quality of parenting.[57] Indeed, some reckon the diminished or disrupted parenting which so often follows marital rupture to be the greatest hazard.[58]

Notwithstanding all these qualifications, the rising rate of divorce and the consequently rising number of single-parent families remain causes for concern. Divorce in itself represents the breakdown of a relationship; and it is a breakdown that will have involved a measure of failure on the part of the couple concerned. Certainly, it is a failure that can be managed more or less well. The damage can be limited. But it would invariably have been better if it could have been avoided in the first place. As a rule, the experience of divorce harms the self-esteem and social confidence of both parents and children. Further, in so far as divorce results in single parenthood, it tends, for a number of reasons, to harm the quality of parenting and to diminish the well-being of children.

There is even some evidence that being a member of a family with only one parent present and active is one of a number of factors that encourage juvenile delinquency. To some extent this is because it is far harder for lone parents – on account of their more limited resources of time and energy, as well as of money – to supervise and discipline their children adequately; and the lack of supervision and the use of immoderate or inconsistent discipline are among the factors most frequently found in the families of children who later become delinquent.[59] Some sociologists are inclined to go further, however, and identify the father's absence or parental inadequacy as the crucial factor. One study has found that of men who by the age of 32–33 in 1980 had avoided becoming an 'offender', 48 per cent had fathers who had been described in 1962 as 'effective and kind'; whereas only 20 per cent of 'offenders' had such fathers.[60] In part, the father's conduct is important simply because it is usually his disappearance that burdens the mother with the heavy demands and limited resources of lone parenthood.[61] But it is also important because male children whose fathers are absent or inadequate lack a (good) role-model, and therefore some clear norm of mature adult manhood to aspire to.[62]

In addition, then, to the direct damage that divorce tends to cause the members of a family ruptured by it, there is also the indirect damage it tends to cause other members of society in so far as it helps to incline some young men to criminal activity. The rising rate of both divorce and crime do give reason for supposing that the capacity of many members of our society to build and maintain friendship – and even to recognize its claims in the first place – is being damaged. They give reason for fearing that the sense of community among us is indeed being diminished, and with it the very fact of community itself.

So we do have a problem. But why? What, as distinct from its symptoms, are its causes?

CAUSES OF DECLINE

Some blame Mrs Thatcher. They hold her responsible for promoting a culture of rampant and avaricious individualism. After all, was it not she who declared in an interview that 'there is no such thing as society'?[63] Well, yes, she did; but, with due respect to those who are wont to find in her the roots of all recent social evil, she did not mean by that remark to deny that individuals have social obligations. In fact, her point was quite the reverse; namely, that individuals should not try to displace their own responsibilities onto society – that is, the government. This is made quite clear elsewhere in the same interview, where Mrs Thatcher is reported as saying that 'the quality of our lives will depend on how much each of us is prepared to take responsibility for ourselves'; and that 'too many people have been given to understand that if they have a problem, it's the government's job to cope with it'.[64] It is also unfair to charge her with trying to promote a greedy, individualistic culture. What she sought to foster was individual responsibility and enterprise, instead of a lazy, complacent, and enervating reliance on the state; and it would be fair to say that she did this primarily in order to promote, not only economic success, but also more vital and more creative community.

Nevertheless, some of Mrs Thatcher's policies have backfired – as she was warned they would. In particular, the contraction of certain kinds of welfare provision, intended to activate the indolent, has often had the effect of rendering the poorest members of society even more helpless and desperate. Thus the governments of recent years have made their own contribution to the decline of community. For, although it is true that

poverty does not invariably lead to marital breakdown, the defi-
cient care of children, and juvenile delinquency – some poor
families have supportive relatives and access to good schools,
and some poor individuals are graced with remarkable moral
strength – it is also true that poverty does encourage these
outcomes. It is widely recognized, not least by married couples,
that financial difficulty poses one of the greatest threats to
marital stability; and in the case of the poor such difficulty is
severe and constant. Further, there is evidence that poverty
tends to undermine good child-rearing practices, such as consistent discipline and parental participation in the play and
educational activities of their children. Even when poor parents know what they ought to be doing, and want to do it, their
social and economic circumstances may make it very hard, if
not impossible, for them to carry it out. As has been observed
in one piece of research:

> the parents were in such poor circumstances that they could
> not put their child-care wisdom into operation. In small
> apartments with thin walls, a premium was often placed on
> keeping the peace so as not to annoy neighbours. So often
> the parents gave in to the children's demands for sweets and
> crisps just for the sake of quiet. The children thus learned
> how to manipulate their parents. Yet at other times, the par-
> ents remained firm. Inconsistency . . . Moreover, the parents
> could rarely afford the books and toys needed to stimulate
> the children nor the fares and entry fees to take them on
> regular family outings. And holidays were almost unknown
> . . . The children then fell behind at school and the parents,
> after early enthusiasm, stopped attending parents' nights
> where they felt inferior to others.[65]

Further still, there is evidence of an association between certain
features of inadequate child-rearing and juvenile delinquency,[66]
and there is reason to suppose this association to be causal.
Therefore, we can infer that, by tending to subvert good childcare, poverty helps to cause delinquency and so to foster criminal activity. Statistics bear out this inference, showing that
delinquents have a tendency to come from low-income and
socially-deprived families: one study of children in the north-east

of England found that 70 per cent of those assessed before the age of five as being both economically deprived and receiving poor domestic care were eventually convicted of a criminal offence.[67]

Some people may be poor because they are not earning enough; but many are poor because they are not earning at all and have not done so for a long time, if ever.[68] These, the long-term unemployed, include older workers who have been made redundant, especially those with no skills or unmarketable ones, and young people who have left school without gaining any qualifications. Not only do such people lack the income to participate in the normal round of social activities that their peers engage in, or to invest in the future; but they also lack the status of being a full, contributing, and worthy member of society, which possession of a job confers.

Unemployment, especially if it is long-term, places considerable strains on marriage and families, not only by creating financial difficulties, but also by removing the customary structure of daily life, challenging traditional assumptions about marital roles and gender identities, and undermining the self-esteem of the unemployed.[69] It also helps to foster criminal activity. By excluding some members of society from many important forms of participation in social life, and from enjoying the benefits of so doing, unemployment helps to weaken their sense of social responsibility.[70] Certainly, it is not the case that there is a direct and simple causal connection between unemployment and anti-social or criminal activity. The crime rate in Britain at the end of the nineteenth century and the beginning of the twentieth was either stable or in decline, while unemployment trends fluctuated (for example, in the 1890s, a period of severe unemployment, the crime rate actually fell); and while unemployment figures in the 1930s were considerably higher than in the 1970s and 1980s, there was no comparable growth of recorded crime.[71] However, if unemployment alone cannot provide *the* explanation for the rise in crime rates since the 1950s, there is nevertheless substantial evidence of a link between long-term unemployment and crime, especially property crime and among young men;[72] and there is good reason to suppose that this link is causal. It is not hard to see, for example, how being unemployed can drive a young man to escape from the depression of boredom and passivity into the excitement and self-assertion of acts of law-breaking.[73] Long-term unemployment may not be *the* cause of rising crime; but, under certain conditions, it becomes *a* powerful force that inclines certain kinds of people toward certain kinds of criminal activity.

According to trans-Atlantic neo-conservative thought since the 1980s, many people have been encouraged to remain unemployed by the excessively generous support of an over-indulgent welfare state; and many couples have been discouraged from marrying by a social security system that makes it more lucrative for mothers and fathers to remain single.[74] Against the first claim, it can be urged that the level of financial reward is not the only consideration that people take into account when deliberating whether or not to take a job or to marry. In defence, however, it can be cogently argued that the financial consideration is likely to weigh very heavily for those whose economic resources are minimal. Against the second claim, it might be objected that while the prospect of being less well-off may incline a couple against getting married, there is no reason to suppose that this decision will, of itself, have an adverse effect on the couple's mutual commitment. But such an argument implies that marriage is merely an act of recognizing a *fait accompli*; which it is not. For in bringing a couple to declare their commitment unconditionally and in public, the act of marriage actually strengthens it – at least, if the bride and bridegroom know what they are doing and take it at all seriously.

Its encouragement of unemployment and its discouragement of marriage are two particular points on which the liberal welfare state has been subject to neo-conservative criticism. More generally, it has been charged with diminishing the individual citizen's sense of responsibility. As the neo-conservative story goes, in seeking to engineer social equality and economic success by trying, for example, to provide unlimited health-care free at the point of service, and to protect employees against unemployment, the paternalist welfare state weakens the individual's inclination to take responsibility for the consequences of their actions. For example, because the state is prepared to pick up the bill for health care, the individual's sense of their own primary responsibility to take good care of their own health (for example, by not smoking), or to take care of an elderly widowed parent, is diminished. And because the state is committed to providing full employment, if necessary by subsidizing uneconomic companies, the individual employee's incentive to work diligently or to moderate wage claims is likewise weakened. Further, since its noble ambitions require it to extend its control over ever more spheres of national life, the welfare state also has the effect of shrinking individual citizens' scope for taking responsibility. For example, because education is entirely in the hands of civil servants, parents have little power to shape how or what their own children are being taught. Exactly how accurate is this diagnosis of our social condition, it is hard to say. The notion that an overindulgent and overcontrolling 'nanny' state infantilizes its citizens is a plausible one; and there is at least anecdotal evidence to suppose that it has done so in our case. Certainly this author has found himself, and heard others, moaning from time to time that the government should be doing 'x' or that the state owes us 'y', when, on reflection, it is not always obvious why the government or the state is assumed to be primarily responsible, or at all.

Some of us, for example, are wont to blame government policy for our social ills. It serves as an easily identifiable scapegoat and implies a relatively straightforward solution: marshal the political power to change public policy, or even to remove the government. But neither the problem nor the solution is really that simple. It is true, as we have pointed out, that there are respects in which government policy has helped to weaken a sense of responsibility, especially among the poorest members of society, but also more generally. Nevertheless, it is a disingenuous overestimate of the power of a democratic government – even one that remains in office for the best part of two decades – to hold it solely or even mainly responsible for determining the moral climate of our society. We must look beyond party politics to deeper cultural forces, forces that we ourselves help to mediate.

One such force is individualism. This is a favourite target of communitarians who take it to be a defining feature of the liberal political vision. By 'individualism' can be meant quite a range of things. At the more theoretical end, it refers to an understanding of human beings as essentially independent of society; and at the more practical end, it refers to a preoccupation with affirming the rights and liberties of individual citizens to the point of obscuring their duties and responsibilities. To what extent such individualism actually is a feature of liberal political theory is a hotly contested issue. One militant apologist for liberalism, Stephen Holmes, argues (somewhat persuasively) that the classic liberal writers all implicitly acknowledged the social constitution of the individual; and that liberal vaunting of the individual's rights and freedoms is not expressive of hostility to community as such, but only of hostility to 'stifling and authoritarian' kinds of community – for example, sects, clans, caste systems and parochial village life. 'Far from being anticommunal,' Holmes writes, 'liberals strove to create a specific kind of community, a community in which citizens enjoyed the cooperation and mutuality made possible by a system of liberal rights.'[75] Nevertheless, even if communitarians are not always fair in their criticisms, and even if they are often not very clear about how political institutions fashioned along non-authoritarian communitarian lines would differ from liberal ones,[76] it does seem necessary to remind many contemporary liberals that the task of limiting the power of the state, of the majority, or of other social bodies to control the aspirations, convictions, or actions of individuals, is not the *only* task necessary to protect and promote social well-being. If it is absolutely right and necessary to secure the individual's freedom from abuse, it is no less so to encourage them to use their freedom in a socially responsible manner. In this respect, communitarians have got it right: there is need to strengthen (somehow) the appeal of social duty.

Irresponsible individualism has been fostered, not only by state paternalism, but also and more fundamentally by the cultural dominance of an egocentric understanding of self-fulfilment. I have argued in Chapter Two that the notion of self-fulfilment is important for making sense of why we do anything, and of why we should or should not do specific things;

and earlier in this chapter I suggested that, in so far as it entails a
fall in our tolerance of abuse, an increase in our attention to self-
fulfilment is no bad thing. However, in so far as self-fulfilment
is understood primarily in terms of the experience of pleasure
— whether physical comfort, sensual excitement, sexual satisfaction, or social success – and in so far as it is connected with an
inability to suffer frustration, disappointment, loss, or injury
for the sake of giving due care to others, then it is corrupt and
destructive. That this hedonistic concept of self-fulfilment is a
force in contemporary youth culture is plain enough to see,
whether in the lyrics of pop songs or the films that Hollywood
produces for the youth market. Exactly what influence this
culture has on the behaviour of its members is very hard to
measure, and impossible to measure with precision. But, aware
of the authority of social norms over adolescent human beings
who are often desperate to be accepted by their peer group,
and aware of the power of the media to generate commonly
held definitions of 'normality', common sense has good reason,
if not hard social scientific evidence, to suppose that the current of hedonism in youth culture militates against the growth
of those virtues of self-control and self-denial that are necessary
if we are to be capable of paying attention to, and sustaining
care for, other people.

On this ground, common sense would go on to say that
hedonism makes a contribution to the preference among
younger people for the limited commitment of cohabitation
over the unconditional commitment of marriage,[77] to the growing tendency of men to withhold themselves from marital
commitment even after they have become fathers,[78] to the rising
rate of marital breakdown, to the relative and absolute absence
of non-residential parents (usually fathers) after divorce, and so
to the cycle of psycho-socially impaired children who grow up
to be unsuccessful spouses and inadequate parents.

Another cultural force that helps to weaken our sense of
social responsibility is the opposite of hedonism, though not of
egocentricity. It idolizes work, not pleasure. Or, to be more
exact, it idolizes professional success. We may call it
'careerism'. To the careerist what matters, in the end, is not the
care of marriage or family or friends or neighbourhood, but

success 'at work'. To some extent, of course, this attitude may be fuelled by the felt need to earn enough to sustain a desired (and sometimes hedonistic) lifestyle. It may also be fuelled by the fact that what is required to secure professional success is often a lot less *personally* demanding that what is required to enable intimate relationships to live and to grow. But to a large extent what drives it is that success 'at work' receives public encouragement and wins overt public applause, whereas success in sustaining and developing various kinds of friendship elicits barely a passing public nod. Our schools, for example, take very seriously the task of preparing us for work. They devote an enormous amount of time to teaching us to add up correctly, to write intelligibly and to read critically. But how much time do they reserve for teaching us (whether in the classroom, on the sportsfield, or in extra-curricular ventures) about the skills necessary to build friendship, what is involved in respecting other people, how to co-operate with them, how to negotiate a conflict, how to choose a marriage-partner wisely, how to keep a marriage alive, and how to bring up children? Under the constraints of the National Curriculum[79] and of the public competition between schools for success in exams, not a lot. Presumably, then, society does not rate this field of knowledge and practice very highly. Or else it considers it so innate or commonplace that normal citizens should not need to be educated in it. Either way the implicit message that society gives its members is that success in relationships deserves as little fore-thought and discipline as it does commendation.

Careerism does not weaken domestic relationships only by diverting most of the careerist's attention and energies into their job. It also does it by requiring them to change job (and often home) frequently – at least once every three years – with the result that being highly mobile is now widely accepted as part of what being a business manager involves.[80] Consequently, according to Dr Tony Munton, research fellow for the Medical Research Council, about a quarter of a million senior managers and their families are moved around every year by UK employers;[81] and according to Michael Schluter and David Lee, what holds in the private sector also holds in the armed services, the NHS, and the Foreign Office.[82] One reason for this high rate of professional mobility is the complexity of the modern organization and of its interdependence with external bodies. This means that whereas '[t]he managerial career may once have looked like a clear and reasonably straight road towards a visible horizon ... now the paths have multiplied. Their courses are increasingly devious, with numerous lateral intersections, and the horizons they lead to are obscured by cloud.'[83] Besides, there are good economic reasons for moving personnel around at a high rate – to broaden their professional experience and their network of contacts. Nevertheless, there are social costs. Friendship takes time and proximity to grow – sometimes even to stay alive. So people who are constantly having to relocate their homes tend to find themselves bereft of intimate friendship: on the one hand, removed from the social network in their previous location; and on the other hand, reluctant to invest themselves fully in their new social location, because they know that they will not be there for long. Of course, many of those who are accustomed to frequent job-moves will have learned how to put down social roots quickly; and no doubt their new professional colleagues will lend a hand. But putting down roots quickly is not the same as putting them down deep. And occasional phone calls and visits are seldom sufficient to keep old friendships vital. Besides, even if adults are skilled at constantly adjusting to new social environments, their children may not be.

One of the cultural forces that fuels careerism, as well as contributing more broadly to marital instability, juvenile delinquency and crime, is the persistent influence of a certain ideal of masculinity. According to this ideal, it is the proper and primary role of the male to support his wife and children by going out into the world to earn money through some form of gainful employment. He is expected to be dominant, at least in his own home, and therefore to be emotionally self-contained, invulnerable, and inexpressive – 'saying nothing, revealing nothing, building a wall of silence between ... [himself] and those who may be able to get at ... [him]'.[84] He is often expected to use physical force to maintain or assert his dominance: in a recent survey, only 37 per cent of men questioned did *not* see violence as an option to be used against their partner.[85] Real men, it seems, are hard men. And since hard men naturally feel at sea in the emotionally delicate and intimate world of child care, they tend to absent themselves: so whereas, on average, full-time working mothers spend twenty-eight hours alone with their children each week, their male partners, also working full-time, manage only six hours.[86] Moreover, their absence is rationalized by a widespread depreciation of domestic life. In her book, *The Trouble with Boys*, Angela Phillips reports of one seven-year-old boy that 'the overwhelming message he receives at school is that people who stay at home with their own children are of less importance in the world than those who go out to work; looking after children is something that only women do'; and she claims, more generally, that 'in two-parent families all over the industrialised world, the preparation for the real world starts with the idealisation of the world outside the home, and the subtle (or not too subtle) denigration of home, mother, and all she stands for'.[87]

By its very nature such an ideal of masculinity is not designed to encourage happy relations between the sexes, or therefore marital harmony, or therefore the decent care of children. What is more, in an era when male unemployment is high, secure full-time work is harder to find, and women are ever more capable of financial independence and ever less willing to tolerate domestic injustice, this role-model for men is becoming increasingly impracticable. And an ideal that continues to be authoritative while not being practicable, can only frustrate and disorient those who are taught to respect it. Could this, then, go some way toward explaining why boys are four times more likely than girls to be labelled as behaviourally and emotionally disturbed; over three times more likely to be registered as drug addicts; and four times more likely to commit suicide?[88] And could it also help to account for the fact that boys are nearly six times more likely than girls to be cautioned or found guilty of an indictable offence?[89] For it is at least psychologically plausible that young males, presented with a socially respectable role-model that they are powerless to imitate, and strongly prejudiced against trying any 'feminine' alternative, should vent their frustration against society by playing 'hard men' outside the rules, whether in the football terraces or on the streets.

Poverty, long-term unemployment, the structure of welfare benefits, state paternalism, individualism, the prevalence of an egocentric notion of self-fulfilment, careerism, high residential mobility, and the persistent influence of a certain ideal of masculinity: these are some of the economic, political and cultural factors that weaken our sense of being responsible for the due care of other members of our society. These are some of the causes of the decline of community among us.[90] What, then, can we do about them?

WHAT CAN WE DO?

There is no simple solution. Since the decline in community is caused by a variety of mutually reinforcing factors, any effective attempt to deal with them would have to operate simultaneously on several different fronts through several different agencies. The solution is complex and comprises a range of remedies.

One appropriate remedy is already fashionable, at least in theory: the promotion of the principle of subsidiarity. Politically, this is the notion that it is the proper task of the state, not so much to do things *for* people as to help them do things for themselves. ('Subsidiarity' derives from the Latin word for help: *subsidium*.) As far as is practicable, particular communities, from the family upwards, should have the responsibility – and the concomitant power – to manage their own affairs. The state's job is to regulate the distribution of resources fairly among the various communities that comprise society, to do what it can to enable those communities to fulfil their responsibilities, and to intervene directly in a community's affairs only in order to prevent the abuse of power or offences against human rights. It may be that there are certain functions that only central government can carry out with the desired level of efficiency. So be it. But the presumption remains that responsibility and power belong at a social level low enough to permit effective participation by the people affected, but at which they can be exercised with adequate efficiency and without creating unacceptable inequalities between the various centres of management. The principle of subsidiarity, of course, applies not only to government, but to any large organization – for example, a business corporation[91] or even a church. What it correctly presupposes is that human beings flourish when they exercise their intelligence with a view to maintaining or promoting goods, including public ones, in the world around them; and that when they feel robbed of the power to do this, then they register their resentment either by being unco-operative or obstructive, or by apathetically withdrawing from the public sphere altogether and burying themselves in their private lives.

One way, then, to foster a sense of social responsibility is to turn paternalistic government – in whatever kind of organization – into enabling government. What this implies for national or central government is that, subject to the requirements of fairness and of a reasonable measure of efficiency, it should give local government responsibility for the management and development of important dimensions of local life, the power to make policy and to fund it to a considerable extent by local taxation, and therefore the need to win and maintain the support of the local electorate.[92] For local government itself to be enabling, it should take as its primary role in the supply of services not that of directly providing them, but rather that of arranging for them to be provided, co-ordinating the providers, and regulating the quality of provision. It may well be that there are certain services of which, or certain conditions in which, local government should be the direct provider. But, even then, if there are other locally-based bodies with relevant interests and expertise, whether private companies or voluntary associations, these should be enabled to involve themselves appropriately in the process of public administration.

Promoting subsidiarity as a principle of all kinds of government and management is one way to foster a sense of social responsibility. Another way is specifically to enable the poor to rise above the daily grind of trying to survive, and to engage in building a worthwhile life – for themselves, their families and their local communities. Wanting to build well, to invest oneself in valuable activity, is a deeply human and vitalizing desire.

Lacking sufficient resources – of money, skill, self-confidence and social support – with which to make such an investment is very frustrating; and lacking hope of ever acquiring these resources is deeply demoralizing. And those who are demoralized by impotence and hopelessness tend to react in one of two ways. Either they blame themselves and become depressed and passive, unable to muster even the will to exercise responsibility over the few things within their control. Or else they blame other people, become hostile, and set about taking revenge (in random acts of violence against the visibly affluent) or seizing what power they can (by property theft or defrauding the welfare system). In a society where most people possess more than is necessary to lead a reasonably comfortable and fulfilling life, where corporate efforts to help those with less than is necessary are mean, and where TV drama and advertising daily parade the extravagant lifestyles of the rich before the eyes of the poor, is it any wonder that some of the needy should find their sense of loyalty to social institutions, of respect for law, and of responsibility to their fellow-citizens strained to breaking-point?

Yes, there is scope for debate about the definition of poverty – about the conditions in which one lacks what is 'necessary' to build a 'worthwhile' life. These conditions are not straightforwardly material, but are complicated by social factors. Nevertheless, the fact that poverty is a complex phenomenon, somewhat relative to prevailing social and economic conditions, does not make it an infinitely flexible notion. Lacking access to a car may or may not help to make you poor, depending on whether you live within walking distance of decent shops and social centres, have neighbours or relatives who will drive you there, or can avail yourself of public transport. But there is no uncertainty about the poverty of those couples with young children, who cannot afford to move out of their cramped two-room flats, whose walls drip with damp, and which are situated in high-rise blocks where the lifts stink of urine and the 'playgrounds' outside have become unofficial rubbish dumps, and in whose crime-ridden vicinities local shops and pubs have long since shut down.

Yes, the poor sometimes bear a measure of responsibility for their own poverty. In which case, let help be extended to them in educational as well as material ways. Yes, the poor do sometimes refuse the aid that is presented them, whether out of depression, apathy, ignorance, diffidence or hostility. So let help be offered with patience and encouragement, and without condescension. And, yes, the 'poor' are sometimes fraudulent, claiming to be unemployed and available for a job while having work in the black market, or claiming to be a single parent while cohabiting with a wage-earning partner. Then let their fraud be exposed and inappropriate help withdrawn.

When all reservations have been considered, and all relevant qualifications made, the original point still stands: that one important way of nurturing a sense of social responsibility is for those who are not poor to give help (one way or another) to those who (really) are.[93] For this will not only enable the poor to assume responsibility; it also gives those who are richer a chance to exercise it, and so to confirm themselves in its virtues.

Certainly, they may do this by private acts of charity. But they should also do it by actively supporting a public system of welfare aid that is supervised, if not entirely administered, by the state. Such a system is preferable to one run purely by private charitable bodies, partly because the state possesses resources of information that enable it to identify most efficiently who the poor really are, and partly because it is one of the state's proper functions to ensure that aid is distributed *fairly* to *all* needy groups and areas within its jurisdiction. In large part, then, richer members of society exercise their social responsibility by consenting to the principle of redistributive taxation, by not defrauding the tax system, and by voting for such increases in tax rates as are necessary to pay for the adequate relief of poverty.

One way to nurture social responsibility is for the state to help support the welfare of the poor – especially those who are long-term unemployed, (single) parents with children, and young people.

The state can help the unemployed by arranging for them to be (re)trained for appropriate work, and by doing what it can to see that such work is available. It can help parents to take good care of their children, for example, by making sure that the tax and benefit systems are more generous to them than to adults without young dependents;[94] by enabling the Social Service and Social Work departments of local government to supply enough day care facilities (thereby allowing parents to work) and family centres (thereby providing them with social support and opportunities for improving their parental skills);[95] and by forcing absentee parents to make a reasonable financial contribution, at least, to the care and upbringing of their children. As regards young people, the state can help by enabling local government to invest in youth work, and especially youth clubs where they can find a stimulating environment and non-delinquent social support.[96]

Of course, all this will cost large sums of money. But it will also save large sums. For by helping to prevent the ill-health, marital failure, delinquency and crime that poverty encourages, it will save society from having to spend considerable resources in trying to cope with their destructive effects. Besides, it will also add immeasurably to the quality of our life together.

Beyond helping the poor, the state can also help to promote social responsibility both by ensuring that the tax and benefit systems do not discourage marriage; and by creating a legal framework designed to limit the psychological and social damage caused by divorce. It could, for example, institute a mandatory waiting period between the making of an application to divorce and its being granted. During this period couples would be required to agree on cash and property settlements, and on arrangements for the care of children. They would also be offered the services of a mediator to help resolve any difficulties.[97] The aim of this procedure would be to remove acrimony from the process of divorce and to prevent subsequent wrangling in the courts, in the hope of making it easier for both adults to continue as active parents and of minimizing the distress caused to the children. It might also, of course, make some people think twice about getting divorced altogether; which would be no bad thing, since there is evidence that many divorced people decide afterwards that they wish they had stayed together.[98]

Aiding the poor, supporting marriage, and reducing the bitterness of irreversible divorce are some of the things that the state can do to help prevent the relationship of parental couples from disintegrating, and the subsequent degeneration of their children into delinquency and crime. But what can it do with those members of society who have already become accustomed to criminal law-breaking? More specifically, what to do with the teenagers who commit the vast majority of instances of burglary and theft, which comprise the bulk of crimes against strangers?[99] And, most specifically, what to do with the 8 per cent of young offenders who commit 80 per cent of detected property crime? For, as Roger Graef says in his well-received book, *Living Dangerously: Young Offenders in their own Words*, 'if we were able to find a way of diverting this small group from the habit of persistent offending, the crime rate would fall dramatically'.[100]

Clearly, prison is not the answer. Two-thirds of ex-prisoners are re-convicted within two years of leaving gaol, and in the case of offenders aged under twenty-one the proportion rises to three-quarters.[101] After interviewing judges and magistrates of a wide spectrum of political views in 1990, Graef found that 'they all agreed that prison was virtually useless as a means to stop re-offending'.[102] And yet the prison population in England and Wales is the highest in Europe, and includes 15,000 young offenders.[103]

But what better alternative is there? A large part of the answer, according to Graef, lies in intensive probation programmes. A model programme of this kind is the Day Centre Course at Sherborne House, in London, where convicted offenders are involved in a full-time, tightly-structured, ten-week course of daily group-discussions about offending behaviour. This involves a series of psychological exercises which disclose the values behind the participants' actions, appeal to their own innate sense of right and wrong, and use group-pressure to back that appeal. Its basic presupposition is that most crimes are the result of choices shaped by inverted value-systems and peer pressure.[104] Such research as has been done – including Graef's own – suggests that programmes like this are considerably more effective than prison at reducing both the frequency and the seriousness of re-offending. They are also cheaper: in 1992 maintaining a place for a year at Sherborne House cost £8,000, whereas a year's place in prison cost £20,000. But although there are 15,000 young offenders, Sherborne House can only accommodate 28 of them for a maximum of 10 weeks. It is the only full-time programme in the whole of Greater London and, according to a Home Office estimate, there are no more than 100 other intensive probation programmes in all of England and Wales, and few of them are as rigorous. As Graef says: 'Of our total expenditure on police, courts, and prisons, we spend less than 1 per cent on all forms of crime prevention. If we really want to achieve law and order and maintain the Queen's peace, our spending priorities are upside down.'[105] For the sake of repairing community, we ought to reverse them. And, who knows, if we were to stop scapegoating the more wayward members of our own society and start shouldering our responsibility for them, then maybe they would begin to recognize their responsibility to us.

There remains at least one more way in which government can help nurture that sense of social responsibility which is the binding force of community: by requiring schools to include social education in their curricula, *and* by enabling them to give it adequate attention. Schools have a vital educational contribution to make in encouraging and helping young people to reflect on and talk about friendship, what it takes to build and sustain it, the different kinds of love, the need for vulnerability and curiosity, the skills of dialogue, how to fight fairly and make conflict fruitful, what gender identities and norms of adulthood are available and which are admirable, and what are the benefits and requirements of investing in marriage and parenthood. Some people might argue that skills in relating to others are mainly and best taught by example and learned by experience, and that mere discussion about them will have little effect. That is probably true. But social education in school need not be confined to the classroom. It can also take the form of extra-curricular activities designed, for example, to foster teamwork. Even so, it is nevertheless valuable to spend time learning to reflect on how we conduct our relationships, and to allow our reflections to be shaped in conversation by the questions and the experience of others. 'But surely,' some might say, 'the family, not the school, is the proper forum for such conversation?' Certainly, it is one possible forum. But many families are not, in fact, very communicative about intimate or delicate matters; and what they do communicate may not be at all helpful. Besides, why not have more than one forum, and let the young learn from both family and school? Since Britain has the highest divorce rate in Europe, and since poor communication is one of the main factors in marital breakdown, anything that we can do to improve our skills in relating to other people – including that of talking about how we relate – has to be a step forward.[106]

So far, the only remedies of community's decline that we have considered are those that local and central government should provide. But government action, though necessary, is by no means sufficient. The contributions of private bodies and individuals are also needed.

For example, employers, private as well as public, need to reconsider the fashionable policy of reducing the number of full-time employees while maintaining the total workload they are expected to bear. Such 'downsizing' may appear to be 'efficient', since it lowers labour costs and increases productivity. But in so far as it results in employees working such long hours[107] that they have almost no time or energy left to invest in other spheres of life – relationships with family-members, for example – this strategy will prove counter-productive. For few people are content to live for their work alone; and overworked, discontented employees are not the most efficient. Indeed, a recent report from the Families and Work Institute in New York found that 'the most important indicator of performance in the workplace is the response of employers to families and their needs'.[108] And Peter Senge predicts a growing trend within organizations to reduce the pressure and demands that make balancing work and family so burdensome; partly because family issues are spilling over much more into managers' lives, since there is increasingly no one else at home to whom such matters can be delegated; but also because of a growing recognition that there is 'a natural connection' between the work dimension of a person's life and all the other dimensions.[109] According to Charles Handy, some employers are already convinced that their employees are actually more efficient if their lives are balanced with a range of interests and commitments than if they are built entirely around work, and therefore deliberately encourage them to get involved in voluntary activities in the community, to sit on public bodies, or to stand for political office.[110] In practice, what such balance requires are flexible working arrangements – including part-time work,[111] job-sharing, flexible working hours, working at home, and extended time off.[112]

The reform of certain structures and policies, whether of (economic) organizations, schools, the penal system, or local and central government would help to improve the health of community among us. Such reforms would do much to help 'normalize' the value of friendship, and so encourage a sense of social responsibility. But they are not enough. For changes in institutions and policies do not automatically issue in corresponding changes in the prevailing assumptions and attitudes of individuals. These are also heavily influenced by such things as the opinions and lifestyles of the 'stars' of the media, and of popular music, film, fiction and sport. So another way to foster healthy community would be for professional critics of culture to publicly challenge such popular 'authorities' when they appear to promote, for example, an egocentric or hedonistic vision of human self-fulfilment, or a destructive ideal of masculinity. Journalists, dramatists, satirists, story-tellers and academics need to exercise their social responsibility to help their fellow-citizens reflect critically upon those values and moral assumptions that are in the cultural air and claim the authority of normality. For some of these exploit human desires and fears, sometimes for political or commercial purposes; and they do so in such a way as to discourage us from growing in those virtues that make us capable of that careful respect for other people which friendship requires.

In the final analysis, however, the health of community depends no more exclusively on the critical outpourings of intellectuals than it does on the decisions of business managers, civil servants, legislators or government ministers. These are important, indeed very important, but they are still not enough. For, as George Eliot wrote, 'the growing good of the world is partly dependent on unhistoric acts; and that things are not so ill with you and me as they might have been, is half owing to the number who lived faithfully a hidden life, and rest in unvisited tombs'.[113] The health of community among us cannot simply be engineered from on high, but depends in large part on the daily decisions and uncelebrated commitments that ordinary citizens make and sustain. It depends on ordinary individuals investing themselves in the good of various forms of friendship, and deciding to let their conduct be governed by its needs, trusting that, whatever its service costs them, they will be the richer for it in the end.

Even, perhaps, in the End.

9

TO WHOM SHALL WE TURN?
THE QUESTIONS OF
MORAL EDUCATION AND AUTHORITY

On 24 November 1993, two eleven-year-old boys became the youngest convicted murderers in Britain for almost two hundred and fifty years, when a jury found them guilty of abducting a two-year-old, James Bulger, and bludgeoning him to death. Their conviction provoked a (brief) period of national soul-searching, led by a flurry of articles in the press trying to grasp the meaning of what had happened, musing about the nature of wickedness, considering the extent to which 'society' should be held responsible for the actions of two of its juvenile members, and generally lamenting the moral decline of late-twentieth century Britain.

The following day a government minister, speaking at a conference on juvenile crime, used the occasion to lay part of the blame at the feet of the Christian churches who, he said, had been 'strangely silent' on moral matters: 'It is surely part of the problem, that while the Church spends its time discussing social issues, such as housing, politicians are left to talk about the importance of the difference between right and wrong.' He went on to say that, in his ten years as a Member of Parliament, there had been no national campaign by the churches to teach children about issues of right and wrong.[1]

But can morality really be taught? If so, how? And who should be doing the teaching?

At one level, morality is not so much taught as recognized. Human beings naturally 'see' the value of things like friendship or knowing the truth or being reasonable. We instinctively know them to be realities that will cause us to flourish if we invest in them. That is, we recognize them as human goods.

'We', here, encompasses all of humankind. The goods are recognized universally. They belong to human nature before they are refracted through human cultures; and only because that is so, do members of a particular culture have any ground upon which to dissent from its moral norms.

Nevertheless, human cultures do develop different sets of insights into the nature of human goods and what investment in them requires. They communicate to their members somewhat different assumptions about what, say, friendship or being reasonable involves. They teach somewhat different norms. So, at a less than basic level, morality is indeed taught.

But how?

Not primarily by the promulgation of some equivalent of the Ten Commandments. Certainly, a moral code can be useful as a memorable summary-statement of the main principles and general rules of a morality; as a starting-point for further reflection and discussion; and as a heartening public expression and affirmation – a public symbol – of moral consensus. But that is all.

One thing that a moral code cannot do, by itself, is to answer the sometimes very complicated question of how a general rule applies in a particular case. For example, granted that we should love our neighbour, does that mean that we should always give money to beggars on the street? And granted that we should not murder, does that mean that we should not experiment with human embryos with a view to improving the success-rate of fertility treatment for couples who desperately need (want?) children? And so on. Questions such as these need illumination by minds that are well-equipped with the tools of analysis and well-trained in its arts. Here, then, a moral code needs to be supplemented by expert lectures and sermons, writing and discussion.

Moral analysis, however, is even less inspiring than moral law. It may shed light on what we should do; but it will not much move us to do it. What can so move us are good stories. Stories of men and women who have responded to the call of human goods, who have let their lives be directed by what is required to invest in them, and who have courageously borne the cost. Such stories might be fact or they might be fiction. Good fiction is not simply untrue: it may not tell us what actually did happen, but it does tell us, plausibly, what could have happened or what might happen yet. And morally moving stories need not be simplistic, moralistic fairy-tales, presenting heroes or heroines as cardboard cut-out saints or as sinners whose road to salvation is strewn with clichés. Indeed, the less they do that, the more able will they be to speak an encouraging word of hope to the messy, confused and inconsistent lives of their typical audience.

If good stories about historical figures or fictional characters can make a powerful moral impression on us, how much more so the direct experience of living persons. First and foremost, it is through the behaviour of other people, especially those we are naturally or socially disposed to trust and respect, that we come to recognize or mistake what is valuable and how to invest ourselves in it. There, above all, in the faces and gestures, the reactions and habits, the decisions and commitments of authority-figures is the beauty of human flourishing revealed or obscured.[2]

Through personal examples, through stories, through analytical lectures and sermons and writing and discussion, and through moral codes, morality can be taught – or, better, light can be cast on what is valuable and how our lives can show due appreciation. But who is responsible for teaching us? To whom should we turn for illumination?

According to the government minister quoted earlier, the answer is straightforward: the Christian churches. From one point of view, his choice is not surprising. Historically, the Christian churches in Britain – and, since the Reformation, especially the established Churches of England and Scotland – have long understood themselves to be the guardians of morality, and have been widely regarded as such; and even today no other social institution yet rivals them in carrying that mantle. However, given the dramatic fall in church membership since the Second World War,[3] and given the growth in public respectability and popularity of alternative religious and non-religious beliefs, it is not clear what moral authority

Christian churches can reasonably be expected to wield nowadays. Perhaps the churches have been speaking; it's just that non-Christians haven't been listening.

And why should they?

Were it the case that the morality espoused by the churches is peculiarly Christian in all its aspects, were it the case that it makes sense only on the basis of peculiarly Christian beliefs about God, then it could have little relevance or appeal to non-Christians. But this is not so. Christian morals do not depend at every point and entirely on Christian faith. Nor is all the content of Christian faith exclusively Christian.

For example, it belongs to Christian faith to believe that reality is fundamentally and ultimately spiritual and not just material; that there exists a personal God, who created and sustains the universe, and who loves his creatures; that human woes are basically a product of alienation from this God; and that human well-being is ultimately secured by overcoming this alienation. These are among the beliefs of Christians. They are also among the beliefs of, for example, Jews and Muslims. Not everything that belongs to the faith of Christians, belongs to it alone. So even if Christian morality did make sense only in terms of Christian faith, it could still make some sense to certain non-Christians.

But not all of Christian morality does make sense only in terms of Christian faith. Christians believe that what makes an action right or wrong is whether or not it promotes, or at least avoids damaging, human goods – including such things as life, friendship and knowledge of the truth. These goods are simply given. Certainly, for Christians, they are ultimately given by God in his act of creation. But, having been given by God, they are also 'given' in the sense that they are *just there* – there as the basic reasons for human action, and there to be grasped by human reflection. Note: *human*, not just *Christian*.

The fact that these goods are *there*, given in and with the world of human inhabiting, explains why it is that Christians are not the only ones who regard murder, injustice and lying as wrong, and who reckon it worthwhile to engage in medical practice, campaigns to free the innocent from prison, and academic research.

Now, of course, this consensus at the level of moral general-ities covers a multitude of more specific disagreements – for example: Is the killing of an unborn child an act of murder? Is a human life that is bereft of all or most of its specifically per-sonal qualities, whether by old age or handicap, still a good worth preserving? Is war always unjust? Should punishment aim to make the criminal suffer? Should those convicted of assassinating fellow-citizens in the pursuit of a political cause be treated as prisoners-of-war and released after peace has been settled? Might it ever be moral to tell a lie to protect the innocent or to avoid pointless distress? The list of controversial moral issues is long; and it probably always has been. But, for our purposes, the important point to note is that the lines of disagreement do not neatly divide Christians from non-Christians. On the contrary, both Christians and non-Christians are to be found on both sides of virtually every moral divide. The significance of this is that it shows that faith or unfaith are not the *sole* determinants of what moral positions we assume.

This is not to say, however, that religious belief makes no moral difference. At some points it certainly does. For example, belief in an after-life where the well-being of the virtuous will be fulfilled makes intelligible an act in which someone surren-ders their life for the sake of standing by the truth or by justice. And belief that there is at work in history a benevolent divine power strong enough to bend evil effects to the service of good ends, strengthens the resolve of human believers never to try to deflect those effects by immoral means. At certain points religious beliefs do alter the context of moral life in such a way as to give good or better grounds for certain kinds of action that otherwise would lack them. But there are many kinds of action whose moral justification requires no (immediate) appeal to the existence of a providential God or to that of an after-life. Instead, it requires only appeal to human experience and reason. Therefore, it is possible for Christian churches to utter moral statements that immediately seem reasonable and persuasive to non-Christians.

But whether or not this possibility is realized does not depend only on appeal being made to common experience or to the common rules and roots of reason. It also depends on the manner in which such statements are made. There may have been a time when the public status of the established Churches of England and Scotland was such that they could relate to the rest of society simply as teacher to taught. There may have been a time when the public granted them a hearing as much because of who was speaking as because of the cogency of what they had to say. There may have been such a time; although, of course, it is one thing to grant a hearing and quite another to heed what is heard. Still, whatever the situation in the past, it is no longer the case that church leaders can stand up to say something and expect, as a matter of course, to hold the public's attention. This is not only because of the apparently diminished plausibility of Christianity in modern times. It is also because people are far less deferential to 'authority' in general. If they are not convinced, they are much more likely than in the past to say so. They are far less inclined to take on trust whatever is said by an authority, especially by a religious authority. What this means is that the churches need to work hard to convince. Before they presume to deliver answers, they need to show that they really have understood the questions, and understood them in all their complexity and awkwardness. If they would become effective teachers, then they must first become – and remain – exemplary students.[4] In the churches' case, as in everyone else's, 'the ear must be opened before the mouth'.[5]

In other words, the churches need to adopt a dialogical manner, drawing alongside others in a common attentiveness to the truth, willing to learn and ready to admit error. This precisely does *not* mean that they should abandon their own convictions, and blandly affirm whatever others are saying. For there can be no serious dialogue unless those taking part have something substantive of their own to say and are willing to say it.

So, even in a society that is religiously and philosophically plural, Christian churches could have something to say about morality that non-Christians would find persuasive. And, as trustees of a set of rich and sophisticated moral traditions (upon which liberal western culture still draws far more than it realizes), the churches have a duty to use their resources in the attempt to shed light on contemporary moral perplexities, and to expose contemporary moral untruths.

But in order to throw effective light, they will need to be prepared to rework their inheritance in response to the novelties of the contemporary world – new problems, new delusions, new data and new insights. And sometimes this reworking will be quite far-reaching and laborious. It will take time. And during this time, there will be much disagreement within the churches and much uncertainty. It will be difficult for them to 'speak out' with confidence. They will not be able to meet journalists' demands for 'answers' to 'problems'. And they will have to suffer accusations from politicians that they have failed to 'teach right and wrong'. But rather than pretending to be in control by trotting out obsolete certainties or launching new ones prematurely, the churches should be content to play pilgrim. If they really feel like being prophetic, they could always respond to demands for a 'statement' by saying something outrageous like, 'We don't know right now; but we're working on it.' They could answer a question by posing a more penetrating one. They could bear witness to what they believe by being modest, candid, patient and careful in what they say – and occasionally even by keeping silence.

In times of moral perplexity, and even in a society that sports a range of world-views, it is fair to expect the Christian churches to play a substantial part in the task of illuminating the moral issues of the day.[6] But that responsibility does not fall on the churches alone. It falls on anyone who possesses the power to influence the shape of the moral world in which we live. And among those who have considerable power in this regard are intellectuals; for these have special skills in thinking beyond appearances, and in communicating what they think to a wider world. This is especially true of those who are able to have their opinions broadcast in newspapers, on TV or on radio.

It is notable, then, that in some of the reflections provoked by the Bulger case intellectuals themselves came under fire – and from among their own ranks. In the wake of the murder, *The Independent* newspaper published an article that was written by Robert Skidelsky, an eminent political historian and biographer, and which was entitled, 'Philosophers can't teach us morals'.[7] In this piece, Skidelsky tells us that intellectuals are good at analysing issues and criticizing opinions, but hopeless at constructing solutions. Since the Enlightenment they have devoted themselves to attacking established (Christian) beliefs and practices in the name of reason and progress. In the course of this project of demolition, however, it began to dawn on some that the values they were fighting for depended on the very foundations they were gaily knocking down. Skidelsky quotes John Maynard Keynes, speaking toward the end of his life (he died in 1946): 'I begin to see that our generation . . . owed a great deal to our fathers' religion. And the young . . . who are brought up without it will never get so much out of life. They're trivial: like dogs in their lusts. We had the best of both worlds. We destroyed Christianity and yet had its benefits.' Fifty years on, Skidelsky reckons Keynes' judgement right:

> [for t]he critical project has yielded not new truths to replace old falsehoods, but value relativism – the doctrine that there is no truth, that everything is a matter of opinion. The 'deconstruction' of all 'discourses', traditional as well as revolutionary, is the final expression of a project that no longer believes in anything or hopes for anything, but simply hates whatever still works, however badly.

This last remark implies that the destructiveness of some modern intellectuals is not simply the unfortunate result of their relentlessly honest and courageous criticism of comforting illusions. It suggests that it is in part due to a certain wilfulness; and, indeed, this hint grows into an unambiguous statement when Skidelsky, paraphrasing Joseph Schumpeter, comments that 'cut off from direct responsibility for practical affairs, the intellectual's main chance to assert himself lies in his actual or potential nuisance value'.[8] The picture he draws, then, is not one of the intellectual hero nobly devoted to the service of Truth, however uncongenial. Rather, it depicts a vain adolescent who, lusting for the limelight, makes a career out of intellectual vandalism.

Skidelsky's remarkable criticism of 'the intellectual class' (remarkable, because he is an eminent member of it) finds a sharp echo in Norman Dennis's scathing account of how and why, since the 1960s, 'the conformist social affairs intelligentsia' have consistently dismissed cries that crime was rising or that the family was breaking down, and have done so in the face of the experience of the ordinary people who have been directly suffering the effects of both. Also paraphrasing Schumpeter, Dennis, too, identifies a strong non-rational motive behind the 'conforming intellectuals'' attack on 'common sense': namely, 'their personal interests in untrammelled self-expression, fame, and money'.[9]

In so far as (some) intellectuals have been guilty of the charges that Skidelsky and Dennis make, then they have not been merely unhelpful; they have been positively irresponsible. For their criticism of received wisdom has not simply been driven by the requirements of reason. It has been fuelled to a notable extent by self-regarding motives, not least the desire to win public applause by conforming to the fashionable image of the anti-establishment iconoclast. As a consequence, their criticism has tended to be indiscriminate, and they have tended not to regard the work of reconstruction as a proper part of their professional brief.

What this implies, however, is not that intellectuals *cannot* help, but that they have often *chosen* not to be helpful. They could choose otherwise. They could choose to search out the truth, even if it means that they have to appear unfashionable. In this search, they could choose to practise dialogue. They could choose to pay attention to the experience of ordinary people. They could choose (unlike Lord Skidelsky) to recognize and engage with the many modern intellectuals who are not predisposed to reject the religious and moral legacy of the past, and who even find much in it that makes good sense. And if they find that the ideas they are disseminating are robbing people around them not only of false hopes but of all hope, and not only of ill-founded meaning but of meaning altogether, and if they care at all for human well-being, then the least they could choose to do is to take the trouble to think again. What they certainly should not do is to imitate the staggeringly complacent shrug of the verbal shoulders with which Skidelsky ends his article: 'For my part,' he writes, 'I remain an intellectual of our times, clinging to the faiths of my generation, knowing they may be false, but having nothing better to put in their place.'

Intellectuals, as well as churches, bear responsibility for the moral state of society. So do those who work in the media. It is sometimes claimed that the media do not shape society, but merely reflect it. This is disingenuous. Certainly, it is true that the media do not simply determine public opinion. We do, after all, choose which newspapers to read or which TV channel to watch; and we do not have to agree with whatever they say. Besides, many editors and directors permit, even solicit, a range of opinion to be published and broadcast. Nevertheless, the media do have considerable power to shape our perspective upon the world. Not just our specific opinions and particular judgements; but also, more broadly, the ideas we take for granted, the awkward facts or aspects to which we are habitually blind, and influential notions of what society or 'everyone else' thinks – influential notions of 'normality'. Since they have this power to shape – not to determine, but still to shape – how we see things, they also have the moral responsibility to use it well.

What might this mean? Part of what it means is that they should aim to do more than give their readers or listeners what (according to the editors) they want, in order to maintain or boost sales or ratings. Newspapers and (most) TV and radio companies are, of course, commercial ventures. They have to attract a readership or audience to make sales and win advertising; and if they do not sell enough newspapers or advertising space, then they will collapse financially and vanish from the scene. True, there may be occasions *in extremis* when it would be better to go under than stay afloat – if staying afloat means that editors and journalists have to pander, for example, to prevalent fascist or racist opinion or to the requirements of government propaganda. There may be occasions when allowing oneself to die is the only way left of saying what needs to be said. Sometimes, then, the imperative to survive should be resisted. Most of the time, however, it can be obeyed without selling one's soul. Most of the time a readership or audience can be maintained or increased without simply confirming its prejudices or exploiting its appetites – whether for sexual titillation, money, vengeance or a sense of moral superiority. If the arts of persuasion are skilfully employed, then readers can be eased from one way of looking at things to another. Or, at least, they can be coaxed to reflect upon some of their assumptions, to pay attention to some of the things they overlook, to wonder who really constitutes 'everyone' and who it is that defines 'normality'. There are ways of inviting people to look in an unfamiliar direction, and to persuade, not alienate, them.

In order to use well their power to shape how we see things, the media need to be concerned about helping us to see things better. Sometimes, that will mean ensuring that a range of (reasonable) opinion is published. Sometimes, it will mean pushing a (worthwhile) line of thought that is neglected or side-lined in public debate – giving voice to the (genuinely) voiceless. The media have a responsibility to stimulate and advance public dialogue. And that is a moral responsibility; partly because serious dialogue presupposes the value of knowing the truth; partly because it involves the exercise of a range of virtues; and partly because it creates co-operative community in spite of differences of opinion.[10]

So far, the kinds of people to whom we have attributed responsibility for the moral state of society are those with special expertise in traditions of moral discussion, religious and otherwise; those with special skills in articulating moral points of view; and those with special power to determine what gets broadcast or not. In brief, they are the kinds of people who specialize in ideas and arguments, and in their communication.

It is arguable that our account so far has been too 'idealist'; that it overestimates the extent to which the moral character of a society is formed by ideas imposed from above. For, as was suggested earlier, we do not learn our moral values or rules primarily from pulpits, or books, or newspapers, or programmes on TV or radio. We learn them not so much intellectually, as socially.

Much of what we hold dear or regard as right, at least in our early years, will have been taught us by our families and by the other immediate communities in which we participate.

And they will have been taught us, probably not in the form of lectures, but more implicitly and subtly through the examples of people to whom we naturally look for social role-models, through the common practices of our communities, through the heroes they celebrate, and through the stories of virtue and vice that they are wont to tell. What this means is that it is not just moral theologians or philosophers or editors or journalists who bear responsibility for the moral health of society, but also parents and grandparents, uncles and aunts, teachers and local religious leaders, local councillors and MPs, managers and government officials, directors and government ministers, film or pop or sports stars, and story-tellers in whatever medium. Responsibility does not just lie on the shoulders of those who deal in (moral) ideas.

Nevertheless, it does lie with them, too. For human beings should not always accept whatever values and rules are given them by society. They should not invariably endorse common practices or admire traditional heroes. They should not necessarily accept moral conventions. Sometimes they should criticize. Sometimes they should rebel. Sometimes they should reject what is given. And they should do so because faithfulness to the Truth that transcends culture requires it. So those who are skilled in the arts of critical reflection have a very important part to play in monitoring and evaluating the moral legacy that society bequeathes us – its role-models, heroes, conventions, rules, codes and values.

But that is not to say that we should look to philosophers, theologians and other intellectuals to simply 'tell' us what is good or right, any more than we should look to parents or teachers or media personalities. Moral wisdom is not the exclusive property of any élite. We cannot therefore evade our own responsibility to seek out wisdom as best we can, by relying indiscriminately on some external authority or other. It may well be that certain persons or bodies or traditions have earned among us the reputation for being especially firm in their moral grasp and especially rich in their moral insights. It may well be, then, that we find them to be authoritative in the sense that we have reason to presume that what they say will be the truth, or something pretty close to it. But to recognize moral authorities in this sense still does not deliver us from the burden and the privilege of having to make judgements for ourselves. Judgements arrived at through dialogue with other people, but our own judgements nonetheless. For, ultimately, we each stand before only one absolute authority: the Truth itself.

We may never see the Truth entire; but that is no excuse for sulkily denying that we can discern it at all. It belongs to our condition as human *creatures* to see as if through a glass darkly. But it belongs to our dignity as *human* creatures to be mindful of what is given us to darkly see.

NOTES

CHAPTER ONE

1. Allan Bloom, *The Closing of the American Mind* (Harmondsworth, Penguin Books, 1988), p. 26. Bloom was a professor of political theory at the University of Chicago until his death in 1992.

2. At the end of the twentieth century, of course, western culture is no longer simply modern (if it ever was), but comprises a mixture of modern and post-modern elements. So while the modern notion of natural scientific knowledge as purely empirical and absolute persists, for example, in much school-teaching, post-modern awareness of its personal, social and metaphysical dimensions flourishes among those who are familiar with contemporary discussion in the philosophy of science.

3. Mary Midgley, *Can't We Make Moral Judgements?* (Bristol, Bristol Press, 1991), p. 125.

4. China rejected western criticisms at the 1993 UN human rights conference in Vienna: see Matthew D'Ancona, 'Nations Cling to Concept of Global Rules on Human Rights', *The Times*, 26 June 1993.

5. See Oliver O'Donovan, *Measure for Measure: Justice in Punishment and the Sentence of Death*, Grove Booklet on Ethics No. 19 (Bramcote, Nottingham, Grove Books, 1977), pp. 21–2.

6. Stephen R. L. Clark, *A Parliament of Souls*, Limits and Renewals 2 (Oxford, Clarendon Press, 1990), p. 21.

7. See James Morris, *Heaven's Command: an Imperial Progress* (Harmondsworth, Penguin, 1979), pp. 71–2, 75–85. According to one reckoning in 1812, 40,000 people were killed each year by the Thugs (p. 78).

CHAPTER TWO

1. F. Nietzsche, *The Gay Science*, Book III, section 130, tr. Walter Kaufmann (New York, Vintage, 1974), p. 185.
2. F. Nietzsche, *Thus Spoke Zarathustra*, Part One, 'Of Voluntary Death', tr. R. J. Hollingdale (Harmondsworth, Penguin, 1961, 1969), p. 98.
3. Nietzsche, *Thus Spoke Zarathustra*, Part One, 'Of Reading and Writing', p. 68.
4. *Fanny and Alexander* (1983) is published on video by Artificial Eye, and distributed by Fox Video.
5. *Crimes and Misdemeanors* (1989) is published on video by Vision Video and distributed by Polygram.
6. Jeannette Winterson, *Written on the Body* (London, Jonathan Cape, 1992), pp. 155–6.
7. Helmuth James von Moltke, *Letters to Freya, 1939–45* (London, Collins Harvill, 1991), p. 412.
8. David Hay, *Exploring Inner Space: Scientists and Religious Experience* (London and Oxford, Mowbray, 1982, 1987).
9. I. Kant, *The Critique of Practical Reason*, Book II, Chapter 2, Section 4, tr. Lewis White Beck, Library of Liberal Arts (New York, Macmillan, 1993), pp. 128–30.
10. Luke 24.11.
11. For a concise argument along these lines, see Thomas V. Morris, *Making Sense of It All: Pascal and the Meaning of Life* (Grand Rapids, Eerdmans, 1992), pp. 173–6.

CHAPTER THREE

1. Milan Kundera, *The Unbearable Lightness of Being* (London and Boston, Faber & Faber, 1985), p. 5.
2. Charles Taylor, *The Ethics of Authenticity* (Cambridge, Mass., Harvard University Press, 1991), p. 39.

CHAPTER FOUR

1. Harrison E. Salisbury, *The 900 Days: the Siege of Leningrad* (New York, Da Capo Press, 1985), p. 463.
2. Alex Duval Smith, 'Giving Up on Life', *The Guardian Weekend*, 13 December 1994, p. 25. The risk of suicide among unem-

ployed men is two to three times greater than that of the average male population (Glenda Cooper, 'As the pop song says, suicide is painless', *The Independent*, 8 August 1995, p. 11).

3. Martin Leighton, *Men at Work* (London, Jill Norman Ltd., 1981), p. 13.
4. Luke 10.30–4.
5. Helen Wilkinson, *No Turning Back: Generations and the Gender-quake* (London, Demos, 1994), p. 16.
6. Wilkinson, *No Turning Back*, p. 16.
7. Wilkinson, *No Turning Back*, p. 16.
8. Wilkinson, *No Turning Back*, p. 16.
9. Wilkinson, *No Turning Back*, p. 16.
10. Wilkinson, *No Turning Back*, pp. 34–5.
11. Wilkinson, *No Turning Back*, pp. 35–6.
12. T. H. White, *The Book of Merlyn* (Austin, Texas, and London, University of Texas Press, 1977), pp. 15–16.
13. Ecclesiastes 9.11–12.
14. Ecclesiastes 2.18–19.

CHAPTER FIVE

1. See Nicholas Saunders, *Ecstasy and the Dance Culture* (London, Neal's Yard DTP Studio, 1995), p. 36.
2. See Augustine, *Confessions,* Book II, 2; III, 1, tr. Henry Chadwick (Oxford, Oxford University Press, 1992), pp. 24–5, 35.
3. The Stoic provenance of this attitude toward sex is one indication that the popular story of puritan, kill-joy Christianity closing down the happy, care-free sexual playground of classical paganism is too simplistic. See Peter Brown, *The Body and Society: Men, Women, and Sexual Renunciation in Early Christianity* (London, Faber & Faber, 1989), Chapter 1, especially p. 21.
4. According to a report made in the TV documentary, *Rave New World*, broadcast on Channel Four in November 1994.
5. *Rave New World.*
6. 'Subway Army' was the name of the hard core of hooligans who used to follow Wolverhampton Wanderers.
7. Sally Weale, 'Foreign Field of Violent Dreams', *The Guardian*, 16 October 1993.
8. Weale, 'Foreign Field'.
9. Bill Buford, *Among the Thugs* (London, Mandarin, 1992), p. 207.
10. Buford, *Among the Thugs*, p. 88.

11. Weale, 'Foreign Field'.
12. Benedict Anderson, *Imagined Communities: Reflections on the Origin and Spread of Nationalism*, revised edn (London and New York, Verso, 1991), pp. 9–12.
13. Emile Durkheim, *The Elementary Forms of Religious Life* (1912).
14. Amos 2.6–8.
15. Amos 9.7.
16. For example, the Samaritan among the ten lepers whom Jesus healed (Luke 17.11–19); the Samaritan woman whom he met at the well (John 4.1–30); and the Gentile centurion who asked Jesus to heal his slave (Luke 7.1–10).
17. Galatians 3.28.
18. Peter Shaffer, *Equus*, in *Three Plays* (Harmondsworth, Penguin, 1976), pp. 258–9.
19. Shaffer, *Equus*, p. 266.
20. Shaffer, *Equus*, p. 210.
21. Shaffer, *Equus*, pp. 274–5.
22. In many forms of religion, of course, moments of heightened religious experience are set, as they should be, in the larger and balancing context of structures of practice that form the whole of life, its mundane days as well as its ecstatic seconds.
23. Peter Shaffer, *The Gift of the Gorgon* (London, Viking, 1993), p. 17.
24. Shaffer, *The Gift of the Gorgon*, pp. 60–1.
25. John 19.34a.
26. Luke 23.34.
27. Luke 23.46.
28. The Apostles' Creed.

CHAPTER SIX

1. Michael Ignatieff, *Blood and Belonging: Journeys into the New Nationalism* (London, BBC Books and Chatto & Windus, 1993), p. 2.
2. One leading sociological analyst of the 'Troubles' in Northern Ireland, Steve Bruce, has arrived at the depressing (though not entirely satisfactory) conclusion that the conflict there is essentially a struggle for ethnic dominance. *The Edge of the Union: the Ulster Loyalist Political Vision* (Oxford, Oxford University Press, 1993), pp. 46, 110.

3. Benedict Anderson, *Imagined Communities: Reflections on the Origin and Spread of Nationalism*, revised edn (London and New York, Verso, 1991), pp. 61–4.
4. Tony Parker, *May the Lord in His Mercy be Kind to Belfast* (London, HarperCollins, 1993), pp. 59–60.
5. Linda Colley, *Britons: Forging the Nation, 1707–1837* (Newhaven, Connecticut, Yale University Press, 1992), p. 368. My emphasis.
6. Briege Duffaud, *A Wreath upon the Dead* (Dublin, Poolbeg, 1993), p. 86. Author's emphasis.
7. Fionnula O'Connor, *In Search of a State: Catholics in Northern Ireland* (Belfast, Blackstaff Press, 1993), pp. 110–11. Partisan selectivity is, of course, quite as typical of the historical memory of Protestants in Northern Ireland as it is of Catholics – as John Dunlop gently implies in *A Precarious Belonging: Presbyterians and the Conflict in Ireland* (Belfast, Blackstaff Press, 1995), p. 24.
8. Peter Shaffer, *The Gift of the Gorgon* (London, Viking, 1993), pp. 15–17.
9. Shaffer, *The Gift of the Gorgon*, pp. 60–1.
10. Shaffer, *The Gift of the Gorgon*, p. 92.
11. Ignatieff, *Blood and Belonging*, pp. 186–7.
12. Yevgeni Yevtushenko, 'Babii Yar', in *The Collected Poems, 1952–90* (Edinburgh, Mainstream Publishing, 1991), pp. 103–4. 'Babii Yar' is the name of a ravine on the outskirts of Kiev where at least 100,000 Jews were massacred in 1941. The massacre was carried out by German troops; but not without the tacit approval of many local Ukrainians, who shared in the long Russian tradition of anti-semitism.

CHAPTER SEVEN

1. Exactly what Pope Pius XII said was: '. . . that which does not correspond with truth or with good morals objectively has no right to exist, to spread, or to be fostered'. To be fair, he also added the qualification that the 'failure to prevent this with civil laws and coercive measures, can be justified in the interests of a higher and more general good'. *Ci riesci*, 6 December 1953, in *Catholic Documents*, XV (September 1954) (London, Pontifical Court Club), p. 16.

2. See Hobbes, *Leviathan*, first published in 1651.

3. The combination is 'covert' in the sense that the materialist metaphysics is often presented as resting on 'scientific' grounds and therefore as carrying the mantle of 'scientific' authority; whereas, in fact, natural science is simply not competent to produce metaphysical judgements about the *ultimate* nature of things.

4. Admittedly, the word 'religious' here is used broadly to include not only experience of the presence of a definite spiritual entity, but also nature-mystical experiences of union of the self with all things.

5. See David Hay, *Exploring Inner Space: Scientists and Religious Experience* (London and Oxford, Mowbray, 1982, 1987), and *Religious Experience Today* (London, Mowbray, 1990).

6. A. J. Ayer, 'Sources of Intolerance', in *On Tolerance*, ed. Susan Mendus and David Edwards (Oxford, Clarendon Press, 1987), p. 92.

7. Theodore Zeldin, 'Why toleration has never been enough', in *An Intimate History of Humanity* (London, Sinclair-Stevenson, 1994), p. 272.

8. Richard Tuck ('Scepticism and Toleration in the Seventeenth Century') and Alan Ryan ('A More Tolerant Hobbes?') both make it clear that scepticism alone is not a sufficient guarantor of toleration, since it can just as easily be used to justify repression for the sake of civil peace – as it was in the sixteenth and seventeenth centuries. See *Justifying Toleration: Conceptual and Historical Perspectives*, ed. Susan Mendus (Cambridge, Cambridge University Press, 1988).

9. Germain Grisez, *The Way of the Lord Jesus*, vol. 2: *Living a Christian Life* (Quincy, Illinois, Franciscan Press, 1993), p. 392.

10. Stephen Holmes, 'The Permanent Structure of Anti-Liberal Thought', in *Liberalism and the Moral Life*, ed. Nancy Rosenblum (Cambridge, Mass., Harvard University Press, 1989), p. 241.

CHAPTER EIGHT

1. This is the judgement of that group of philosophers, political theorists and sociologists which have been labelled 'communitarian'. Perhaps their best known representative is Amitai Etzioni, Professor of Sociology at George Washington University, author of *The Spirit of Community: Rights, Responsibilities,*

and the Communitarian Agenda (New York, Crown Publishers, 1993), and reputed influence upon the US President, Bill Clinton, and the leadership of the British Labour Party under Tony Blair (see 'Freedom and Community', *The Economist*, 24 December 1994 – 6 January 1995, p. 65).

2. Peter Senge, *The Fifth Discipline: the Art and Practice of the Learning Organization* (London, Century Business, 1992, 1990), especially Chapter 12.

3. Senge, *The Fifth Discipline*, pp. 4, 10, 25, 159, 171, 245, 248, 274, 285.

4. Senge, *The Fifth Discipline*, pp. 206, 148–9.

5. Senge, *The Fifth Discipline*, p. 224.

6. Senge talks in terms of managers' need to develop 'personal mastery'. This includes a firm grasp of the values they want to promote; and among these should be the self-respect and the self-actualization of the members of their organization (*The Fifth Discipline*, pp. 7, 8, 140, 144). Clearly, a culture of dialogue will never get off the ground unless managers are patently genuine in their respect for fellow-members.

7. E. M. Forster, *A Passage to India* (1924) (Harmondsworth, Penguin, 1987), p. 245.

8. In Britain a national opinion poll published by *The Observer* in 1993 found that, in rating institutions which could be trusted, the public reckoned the government bottom, and Parliament next to bottom. Cited by Bob Holman in *Children and Crime: How Can Society Turn Back the Tide of Delinquency?* (Oxford, Lion, 1995), p. 52.

9. Although even this is likely to be less than entirely accurate, since some victims – e.g., battered wives – probably do not admit their experience to interviewers.

10. 3 January 1995.

11. *The Economist*, 7 January 1995, pp. 20–1.

12. *The Economist*, 7 January 1995, p. 21.

13. *The Economist*, 7 January 1995, p. 21.

14. Pat Mayhew, Catriona Mirrlees-Black, and Natalie Aye Maung, 'Trends in Crime from the 1994 British Crime Survey', Research Findings 14 (London, Home Office Research & Statistics Department, September 1994).

15. P. Mayhew, D. Elliot, and L. Dowds, *The 1988 British Crime Survey*, Home Office Research Study 111 (London, HMSO, 1989), pp. 13, 15.

16. *The Economist*, 7 January 1995, p. 20.

17. Scotland has also enjoyed a recent fall in recorded crime of about 11 per cent between 1991 and 1994, as have several other countries, including the USA, where crime fell by about 4.9 per cent between 1991 and 1993. See *Criminal Statistics 1994* (London, HMSO, 1995), p. 23, Table 1.2.

18. See 'Notifiable Offences, England & Wales, July 1994 to June 1995', *Home Office Statistical Bulletin*, 19/95 (London, Home Office Research & Statistics Department, September 1995).

19. *The Economist*, 7 January 1995, p. 21.

20. The Henley Centre for Forecasting 1992, as reported by Norman Dennis and George Erdos in *Families without Fatherhood*, Choice in Welfare Series No. 12, second edn (London, IEA Health and Welfare Unit, 1992), p. 77.

21. David Utting, *Family and Parenthood: Supporting Families, Preventing Breakdown* (York, Joseph Rowntree Foundation, 1995), p. 14.

22. Utting, *Family and Parenthood*, p. 15.

23. Utting, *Family and Parenthood*, p. 19.

24. J. Haskey, 'Current prospects for the proportion of marriages ending in divorce', *Population Trends*, 55 (London, OPCS/HMSO, 1989).

25. Utting, *Family and Parenthood*, p. 30 n.47.

26. Jojo Moyes, 'Bed, please, but hold the romance', *The Independent*, 23 January 1995, p. 18.

27. Utting, *Family and Parenthood*, p. 14.

28. Martin Whitfield, 'Marriage figures wreck minister's case', *The Independent*, 15 September 1994, p. 6. See also Nick Buck, Jonathan Gershuny, David Rose, and Jacqueline Scott, *Changing Households: the British Household Panel Survey 1990–92* (Colchester, ESRC Research Centre on Micro Social Change, 1994), pp. 37–44, 74–9.

29. Whitfield, 'Marriage figures'.

30. Buck et al., *Changing Households*, p. 61. See also pp. 62, 79–82.

31. J. Haskey, 'Pre-marital Cohabitation and the Probability of Subsequent Divorce: Analyses using new data from the General Household Survey', *Population Trends*, 68 (Summer 1992), p. 10. Buck et al., *Changing Households*, pp. 61–2, 79–82.

32. Zelda West-Meads, 'Why an experiment in matrimony often ends in acrimonious divorce', *The Independent on Sunday*, 21 June 1992.

33. R. Phillips, *Putting Asunder: a History of Divorce in Western Society* (Cambridge, Cambridge University Press, 1988), p. 639.

34. 'Family Values', *The Economist*, 26 December 1992 – 8 January 1993, p. 67.

35. H. Carter and P. Glick, *Marriage and Divorce: a Social and Economic Study* (Cambridge, Mass., Harvard University Press, 1970), p. 345.

36. Jack Dominian, Penny Mansfield, Duncan Dormor, and Fiona McAllister, *Marital Breakdown and the Health of the Nation* (London, One plus One, 1991), p. 17.

37. S. Platt, K. Hawton, N. Kreitman, J. Fagg, and J. Foster, 'Recent clinical and epidemiological trends in parasuicide in Edinburgh and Oxford: a Tale of Two Cities', *Psychological Medicine*, 18 (1988), p. 405.

38. 'Family Values', *The Economist*, p. 67.

39. In 1992 168,248 English and Welsh children under the age of 16 experienced their parents' divorce, more than double the number for 1971. If the trend continues, 1 in 4 children born today will see their parents divorcing before they reach the age of 16 (Utting, *Family and Parenthood*, p. 20).

40. Frank F. Furstenberg and Andrew J. Cherlin, *Divided Families: What Happens to Children when Parents Part* (Cambridge, Mass., Harvard University Press, 1991), pp. 35–6.

41. Polly Toynbee, 'Children who never forgive', *The Observer*, 3 September 1989, p. 34. According to a 1991 study, only 57 per cent of non-resident parents had contact with their children. Of those who had no contact, more than 1 in 4 had never had any at all and almost 1 in 2 had not had any for more than 1 year. J. Bradshaw and J. Miller, *Lone Parent Families in the UK*, DSS Research Report 6 (London, HMSO, 1991), pp. 11–12. According to a 1994 study of 76 children in families 're-ordered' after separation or divorce, for 66 of whom separation had occurred at least 4 years before being interviewed, and for 10 of whom it had occurred less than 4 years before, only 1 in 3 had frequent, regular contact with non-resident parents and 1 in 4 had lost contact altogether. M. Cockett and J. Tripp, *The Exeter Family Study: Family Breakdown and its Impact on Children.* (Exeter, University of Exeter Press, 1994); reported by Utting, *Family and Parenthood*, p. 48.

42. In 1971 there were 1m children in single-parent families; in 1992, there were 2.3m. The proportion had risen from 1 in 13

to about 1 in 5. See J. Haskey, 'Estimated Numbers of One-Parent Families and their Prevalence in Great Britain in 1991', *Population Trends*, 78 (London, OPCS/HMSO, 1994).

43. M. H. King and C. M. Elliott, 'The Diseases of Gods: Some Newer Threats to Health', in *The Oxford Textbook of Medicine*, ed. D. Weatherall, J. G. G. Ledingham, and D. A. Warrell, 2 vols. (Oxford, Oxford University Press, 1995).

44. As reported by Nicholas Ward, 'Professor "shudders for next generation"', *The Times*, 3 July 1991. For sociological documentation, see Michael Schluter and David Lee, *The R Factor* (London, Hodder & Stoughton, 1993), pp. 141, 149.

45. Bradshaw and Miller, *Lone Parent Families*, pp. 20–3, 31.

46. 'Family Values', *The Economist*, p. 67.

47. Ken Judge and Michaela Benzeval, 'Health Inequalities: new concerns about the children of single mothers', *British Medical Journal*, no. 6879, vol. 306 (13 March 1993), pp. 677–80.

48. K. E. Kiernan, 'The Impact of Family Disruption on Transitions Made in Young Adult Life', *Population Studies*, 46 (1992), p. 233.

49. Polly Toynbee summarizing Judith Wallerstein and Sandra Blakeslee, *Second Chances* (London, Corgi Books, 1989), in 'Children who never forgive'.

50. As Louie Burghes concludes from her review of research into the well-being of children growing up in lone-parent families: 'Where disparities in overall outcomes are revealed between children of two-parent intact families and families of different structures – lone-parenthood or reconstituted – these seem to stem less from the family structure or disruption per se and more from the nature of the disruption.' *Lone Parenthood and Family Disruption: the Outcomes for Children*, Occasional Paper 18 (London, Family Policy Studies Centre, 1994), p. 23.

51. Toynbee, 'Children who never forgive'; Ingrid Lund, Institute of Education, London – quoted by Olivia Timbs in 'Divorce is bad for you, try again', *The Independent*, 1 September 1992.

52. M. Rutter and D. J. Smith, eds., *Psychosocial Disorders in Young People: Time Trends and their Causes* (Chichester and New York, John Willey, 1995), p. 783; D. J. West, *Delinquency: its Roots, Careers, and Prospects* (London, Heinemann, 1982), p. 57.

53. Jean L. Richardson, Kathleen Dwyer, Kimberly McGuigan, William Hansen, Clyde Dent, C. Anderson Johnson, Steven Y. Sussman, Bonnie Brannon, and Brian Flay, 'Substance Use

among Eighth-Grade Students who Take Care of Themselves after School', *Pediatrics*, 84/3 (September 1989), pp. 556–66.

54. B. J. Elliot and M. P. M. Richards, 'Children and Divorce: Educational Performance and Behaviour before and after Parental Separation', *International Journal of Law and the Family* 5 (1991), pp. 258–76; A. J. Cherlin, F. F. Furstenberg, P. L. Kiernan, P. K. Robins, D. R. Morrison, and J. O. Teitler, 'Longitudinal Studies of Effects of Divorce on Children in Great Britain and the United States', *Science*, 252 (1991), pp. 1386–9.

55. J. McCord, 'A Longitudinal View of the Relationship between Paternal Absence and Crime', in J. Gunn and D. F. Farrington, eds., *Abnormal Offenders, Delinquency, and the Criminal Justice System* (Chichester and New York, John Wiley, 1982), pp. 113–21.

56. P. R. Amato and B. Keith, 'Parental Divorce and the Well-Being of Children: a Meta-analysis', *Psychological Bulletin*, 110/1 (July 1991), pp. 39–40. See also West, *Delinquency*, p. 55: 'It would seem that family discord is the main reason for the link between broken homes and delinquency.' Rutter and Smith reach the same conclusion about the connection between family break-up and psychosocial disorders in young people (*Psychosocial Disorders*, p. 783).

57. M. P. M. Richards, 'The Interests of Children at Divorce', a paper presented to the 'Families and Justice' International Conference, Brussels, 1994; cited by Utting in *Family and Parenthood*, p. 51.

58. J. Wallerstein and J. Kelly, *Surveying the Breakup: How Children and Parents Cope with Divorce* (London, Grant Macintyre, 1980).

59. Rutter and Smith, *Psychosocial Disorders*, p. 798; D. Utting, J. Bright and C. Henricson, *Crime and the Family: Improving Child-Rearing and Preventing Delinquency* (London, Family Policy Studies Centre, 1993), p. 23. For further discussion of the relationship between inadequate child care and delinquency, see Holman, *Children and Crime*, pp. 25–32.

60. I. Kolvin, F. J. W. Miller, D. M. Scott, S. R. M. Gatzanis, and M. Fleeting, *Continuities of Deprivation: the Newcastle 1000 Family Study*, ESRC/DHSS Studies in Deprivation and Disadvantage 15 (Aldershot, Avebury, 1990), pp. 278–9, Tables 14.5 and 14.6.

61. Dennis and Erdos, *Families without Fatherhood*, pp. 44–5: 'A

frequent argument is that the differentials [in well-being between children with a sociological father and those without] are there, but they are not due to the absence of the father "as such". They are due to the absence of money. But the shortage of money is itself due to the absence of the father.'

62. Dennis observes that the young males who rioted in 1991 on the Meadow Well housing estate in Tyneside 'did not have a taken-for-granted project for life of responsibility for their own wife and children', and rates this as among the most potent factors that encouraged their destructive behaviour (Dennis and Erdos, *Families without Fatherhood*, pp. 107, and 102–8). Elsewhere he writes: 'If we are looking for something that has profoundly changed for young males in the twenty or thirty years during which many of them have gone on the rampage . . . [i]t is in the social definition of what it is to be a mature man.' *Rising Crime and the Dismembered Family: How Conformist Intellectuals have Campaigned against Common Sense*, Choice in Welfare Series No. 18 (London, IEA Health and Welfare Unit, 1993), p. 9.

63. *Women's Own*, 31 October 1987. To be exact, what Mrs Thatcher said was: 'there is no such thing as society: there are only individual men and women, and there are families'.

64. *Women's Own*, 31 October 1987.

65. Holman, *Children and Crime*, pp. 70–1.

66. Holman, *Children and Crime*, pp. 25–32.

67. Holman, *Children and Crime*, pp. 57, 104.

68. On 12 October 1995, according to official government figures, there were 825,700 people in the UK who had been unemployed for 1 year or more; 479,000 for 2 years or more; and 330,000 for 3 years or more. *Employment Gazette*, December 1995 (London, HMSO, 1995), p. S.28, Table 2.8.

69. Jacqueline Burgoyne, 'Unemployment and Married Life', *Unemployment Unit Bulletin*, 18 (November 1985), pp. 7–10.

70. See *Crime and Social Policy*, a report of the Crime and Social Policy Committee of the National Association for the Care and Resettlement of Offenders (London, NACRO, 1995), p. 70.

71. Gertrude Himmelfarb, *The Demoralization of Society: from Victorian Virtues to Modern Values*, Choice in Welfare Series no. 22 (London, IEA Health and Welfare Unit, 1995), p. 238; Dennis and Erdos, *Families without Fatherhood*, pp. 86–7. Dennis notes,

p. 106, that when, in the autumn of 1991, young men rioted on the Meadow Well estate in Tyneside, 87 per cent of the region's working population were employed, and a higher proportion of the adult population was in work then ever before. See also Rutter and Smith, *Psychosocial Disorders*, p. 794: 'The theory that rising unemployment has caused the ... increase [since 1945] in psychosocial disorders [including crime] can be decisively rejected.'

72. *Crime and Social Policy*, pp. 71–2. See also Rutter and Smith, *Psychosocial Disorders*, pp. 795, 783. According to Roger Graef, 'jobs – and the lack of them – are *a* central reason why most young people who commit crime do so in the first place'. *Living Dangerously: Young Offenders in their own Words* (London, HarperCollins, 1992), p. 40. My emphasis. A survey by senior probation officers in 1993 found that 70 per cent of serious offences were committed by the unemployed (Holman, *Children and Crime*, p. 58).

73. See Holman, *Children and Crime*, pp. 60–2.

74. See Charles Murray, *The Emerging British Underclass*, Choice in Welfare Series 2 (London, IEA, 1990); *Underclass: the Crisis Deepens*, Choice in Welfare Series 20 (London, IEA, 1994).

75. Stephen Holmes, 'The Permanent Structure of Antiliberal Thought', in *Liberalism and the Moral Life*, ed. Rosenblum, p. 251. He puts his case more fully in *The Anatomy of Antiliberalism* (Cambridge, Mass., Harvard University Press, 1993). It is significant that Charles Taylor, an eminent communitarian, concedes that not every species of liberalism denies the essentially social nature of the individual. See 'Cross Purposes: the Liberal-Communitarian Debate', in *Liberalism and the Moral Life*, pp. 159–63.

76. As complain the authors of 'Freedom and Community', *The Economist*, 24 December 1994 – 6 January 1995, pp. 65–8; and of 'Communitarian Conceits', *The Economist*, 18 March 1995, pp. 20–1.

77. Utting, *Family and Parenthood*, pp. 15–17.

78. In 1971 under 9 per cent of births occurred outside of marriage; in 1981, 13 per cent; in 1991, more than 30 per cent. Of those babies born outside of marriage during 1992, almost 25 per cent were registered by their mothers alone, and 20 per cent were registered by both parents giving separate addresses (Utting, *Family and Parenthood*, pp. 18–19).

79. The 1988 Education Act requires schools in England and Wales to concern themselves with the moral, spiritual, and cultural well-being of children, and many schools do provide for Personal and Social Education; but the academic requirements of the National Curriculum leave little time for it.

80. N. Nicholson and M. West, *Managerial Job Change: Men and Women in Transition* (Cambridge, Cambridge University Press, 1988), p. 70.

81. As reported by Judy Jones, 'Executives "left to cope with stress when firms move"', *Independent*, 18 October 1991. See Anthony Munton, Nick Forster, Yochanan Altman, and Linda Greeberg, *Job Relocation: Managing People on the Move* (Chichester and New York, John Wiley, 1993), p. 2.

82. Schluter and Lee, *The R Factor*, pp. 126–7.

83. Nicholson and West, *Managerial Job Change*, p. 5.

84. Angela Phillips, *The Trouble with Boys: Parenting the Men of the Future* (London, HarperCollins, 1993), p. 70.

85. Phillips, *The Trouble with Boys*, p. 13.

86. Julia Brannen and Peter Moss, *Managing Mothers: Dual Earner Households after Maternity Leave* (London, Unwin-Hyman, 1991), p. 160, Table 10.1.

87. Phillips, *The Trouble with Boys*, pp. 175, 122.

88. Phillips, *The Trouble with Boys*, pp. 24, 26.

89. Phillips, *The Trouble with Boys*, p. 29.

90. There may well be others; for example, a youth culture that alienates adolescents from adults. As Rutter and Smith write in the conclusion of their collection of studies of the rise in psychosocial disorders in young people since 1945: 'What seems most striking is the growth of a youth culture and of youth markets (for music, fashion and places of entertainment) which mark off adolescents as a separate group in a more decisive way than earlier in the century. These changes . . . may tend to insulate young people from the influence of adults, in particular their parents, and increase the influence of the peer group. It may therefore be that it is an isolated youth culture that leads to the increase in psychosocial disorders. That theory seems worth investigating in future research' (*Psychosocial Disorders*, p. 801).

91. See Charles Handy, *The Empty Raincoat: Making Sense of the Future* (London, Hutchinson, 1994), Chapter 7.

92. It is widely thought that local government in Britain today has far too little autonomy (see, for example, Graham Mather,

'Time to set town halls free', *The Times*, 4 May 1995). Could this be one of the reasons why an unprecedentedly low figure of only 38 per cent of the electorate bothered to turn out to vote in the local elections of May 1995?

93. To say that helping the poor is *useful* in bolstering their sense of social responsibility, is not to deny that such help is also *deserved*.

94. At the moment, British taxpayers with children suffer negative discrimination. In 1994–5 single taxpayers of all categories contributed a lower percentage of their gross earnings in tax and NICs (ranging from 22.2 to 38.4 per cent) than in 1978–9. Likewise, childless married men on average or higher earnings (ranging from 26.8 to 38.3 per cent). But in the case of couples with two children under 11 years old, where only the husband is earning, the direct tax burden increased from 9 per cent of average gross earnings in 1964–5, to 21 per cent in 1978–9, to 32 per cent in 1994–5; from 4 per cent of $^3/_4$ average earnings, to 14.6 per cent, to 17.5 per cent; from 2.2 per cent of $^1/_2$ average earnings, to 2.5 per cent, to 8.8 per cent. Further, since 1977 Child Benefit has kept pace neither with earnings nor with price inflation (see Utting, *Family and Parenthood*, pp. 36–7).

95. Holman, *Children and Crime*, pp. 99–151. The 1989 Children Act, Section 17 (10), holds local authorities responsible 'to safeguard and promote the welfare of children within their area who are in need' by organizing (in partnership with parents, voluntary agencies, and the social, health, housing, and education services) a range of parental support services, especially the provision of neighbourhood family centres. For a review of attempts to implement the Act hitherto, see Utting, *Family and Parenthood*, p. 66.

96. Holman, *Children and Crime*, Chapters 9–10.

97. Proposals to this effect have been made by the Lord Chancellor.

98. According to a survey carried out in Bristol in 1982–4, 51 per cent of men and 29 per cent of women (i.e. an average of 40 per cent) are of this opinion. See Gwynn Davis and Mervyn Murch, *Grounds for Divorce* (Oxford, Clarendon Press, 1988), p. 59.

99. Violent offences make up only 6 per cent of recorded crime, and the victim of a violent crime is often known by the perpetrator (Graef, *Living Dangerously*, p. 1).

100. Graef, *Living Dangerously*, p. 1.
101. Graef, *Living Dangerously*, p. 2.
102. Graef, *Living Dangerously*, p. 2.
103. Graef, *Living Dangerously*, pp. 258–9.
104. Graef, *Living Dangerously*, p. 6.
105. Graef, *Living Dangerously*, p. 259.
106. Utting (*Family and Parenthood*, p. 57) approves of a proposal to begin education about parenthood and family life in, among other places, schools (Gillian Pugh, Erica De'Ath, and Celia Smith, *Confident Parents, Confident Children: Policy and Practice in Parent Education and Support* [London, National Children's Bureau, 1994], pp. 70–2; and the NACRO report, *Crime and Social Policy*, urges the Government to ensure 'that preparation for family life and education on [*sic*] parenting become part of the curriculum of every secondary school in the country' (p. 76).
107. In 1991 23 per cent of employees in Britain worked a six or seven day week. See Patricia Hewitt, *About Time: the Revolution in Work and Family Life* (London, Institute for Public Policy Research/Rivers Oram Press, 1993), p. 23, Figure 1.7.
108. According to Marion Kozak in 'Exit the Man in the Grey Suit', *ChildCare Now*, 13/3 (1993), p. 10, where she reviews the Families and Work Institute's report, *The National Study of the Changing Workforce*.
109. Senge, *The Fifth Discipline*, pp. 307, 311.
110. Handy, *The Empty Raincoat*, p. 72.
111. Helen Wilkinson, *No Turning Back: Generations and the Gender-quake* (London, Demos, 1994), p. 13. In 'The End of Unemployment: Bringing Work Back to Life', *Demos Quarterly*, 2 (1994), Charles Leadbeater and Geoff Mulgan observe that across the European Union three times as many full-timers want to go part-time as vice-versa. Sharon Witherspoon and Gillian Prior in R. Jowell, L. Brook, B. Taylor, with G. Prior, *British Social Attitudes – the 8th Report* (London, Dartmouth, 1991), found that 12 per cent of male, and 11 per cent of female, full-timers would go part-time if they had the option (p. 135). According to Wilkinson, in *No Turning Back*, anecdotal evidence collected by the Equal Opportunities Commission suggests that a significant minority of younger men are actively seeking out part-time, temporary jobs so that they can share their children's upbringing (p. 17).
112. See Kozak, 'Exit the Man', *ChildCare Now*, pp. 10–11.

113. George Eliot, *Middlemarch* (1871-2), ed. Rosemary Ashton (Harmondsworth, Penguin, 1994), p. 838.

CHAPTER NINE

1. *The Independent*, 26 November 1993, p. 2.
2. Therefore, with due respect to the government minister quoted at the beginning of this chapter, efforts by the churches (or anyone else) to alleviate economic and social poverty do make a very important contribution to the promotion of moral education. This is because lack of adequate resources – of material, of skill, and of social support – can so exhaust and demoralize parents and teachers as to make it much harder for them to display the virtues of care, patience, and consistency in their treatment of the young. See Chapter Eight, p. 111.
3. Grace Davie, *Religion in Britain since 1945: Believing without Belonging* (Oxford, Blackwell, 1994), Chapter 4.
4. The Christian churches, above all, should know this. It was one of the recurrent themes of Jesus' teaching and practice that only good servants make good masters (Matthew 20.20-8; John 13.2-17); and good service involves paying close attention to those one seeks to serve.
5. Keith Clements, *Learning to Speak: the Church's Voice in Public Affairs* (Edinburgh, T. & T. Clark, 1995), p. 173.
6. Most of what has been said here about the role of the Christian churches in the moral formation of a 'pluralist' society, could equally well be said of the role of other religious communities, for example, the Jewish and Muslim.
7. *The Independent*, 24 November 1993.
8. Joseph A. Schumpeter, 'The Sociology of the Intellectual', in *Capitalism, Socialism, and Democracy* (London, George Allen & Unwin, 1943, 1976), pp. 145-55.
9. Norman Dennis, *Rising Crime and the Dismembered Family: How Conformist Intellectuals Have Campaigned Against Common Sense*, Choice in Welfare Series No. 18 (London, IEA Health and Welfare Unit, 1993), p. 19.
10. For one recent example of newspapers carrying out their responsibility to foster public dialogue by presenting their readership with uncongenial points of view, take the decision of an Irish nationalist paper in Belfast to publish an article arguing that the political unification of Ireland is not the only

or the best road to a just peace ('Holding gun of unity to unionists' heads', *The Irish News*, 20 August 1994, p. 6), and the decision of a Unionist paper to publish a piece urging Unionists to recognize the legitimate grievances of nationalists and to make concessions ('Time for risk taking to secure the Union', *The Belfast Telegraph*, 7 February 1995, p. 10).

FURTHER READING

Mary Midgley, *Can't We Make Moral Judgements?* (Bristol, Bristol Press, 1991). A lively and accessible discussion of moral relativism by a professional philosopher.

Charles Taylor, *The Ethics of Authenticity* (Cambridge, Mass., Harvard University Press, 1991). Another philosopher engagingly explains why what is arguably *the* modern value, authenticity, need not and should not keep company with moral relativism and nihilism.

Michael Schluter and David Lee, *The R Factor* (London, Hodder & Stoughton, 1993). An economist and a freelance journalist argue that western culture is undermining relationships, and say what should be done about it.

Bob Holman, *Children and Crime: How Can Society Turn Back the Tide of Delinquency?* (Oxford, Lion, 1995). Written by a one-time professor of social administration who was born in London's East End and now lives in Europe's largest housing estate, Easterhouse in Glasgow; and addressed to the concerned citizen who wants to know how to help.

INDEX

Aristotle 98
Augustine 59
authenticity 42–5
authoritarianism 3–4, 11–12
authority 30–3, 132, 135,
  141–2
autonomy, moral 12–14; *see
  also* freedom
Ayer, A. J. 87

Bible: Amos 64; Ecclesiastes
  54–5; Luke 28, 50, 70, 146n;
  John 70, 146n; Galatians
  146n
Bloom, Alan 1
Buford, Bill 61, 62

careerism 116–17
character, building of 20–1,
  52, 55, 98, 116, 123, 128
children, care of 106–9, 116,
  119, 124
choice 41–2
Christian ethics 133–4
Clark, Stephen R. L. 8
cohabitation 104–5, 116
Colley, Linda 75
commitment 37–40

communitarianism 93, 101,
  114–15
community 60–2, 90, Chapter
  8 *passim*, 140
crime 102–3, 113, 120, 125
Crimes & Misdemeanors 19
cultural criticism 128

delinquency, juvenile 109–10,
  111–12, 119–20
Dennis, Norman 138
dependence 36–7, 73
dialogue 8–10, 88–90, 96–7,
  100–1, 135, 140
divorce 103–9, 116, 124
downsizing 127
drugs 57, 68, 69
Duffaud, Briege 75–6
Durkheim, E. 63

ecstasy 46–7, Chapter 5
  passim
education, moral and social:
  Chapter 9 *passim*, 117,
  126–7, 130–2; and the
  churches 132–6; and
  intellectuals 136–9; and the
  media 139–40
Eliot, George 129

Fanny and Alexander 16
football hooliganism 61, 63
forgiveness 69–70, 77–8, 82
Forster, E. M. 99
freedom: Chapter 3 *passim*;
   and connectedness 40; and
   exploration 42
Freud, Sigmund 16
friendship 94–101

gender roles *see* masculinity;
   labour, domestic division of
Graef, Roger 125–6
Grisez, Germain 89–90

Halsey, A. H. 106–7
Handy, Charles 128
happiness *see* self–fulfilment
Hobbes, Thomas 85
Holman, Bob 111
Holmes, Stephen 91, 115

iconoclasm 32, 44, 138
Ignatieff, Michael 71, 81–2
imperialism, moral 3, 4–5,
   9–10
individualism 4, 114–15

Jesus 26, 28–9, 50, 64–5, 70
Jung, Carl 17

Kant, Immanuel 28
Keynes, John Maynard 137
King, M. H. and Elliot, C. M.
   106
Kundera, Milan 39

labour: 48–9; domestic
   division of 50–2; *see also*
   work
legalism, moral 3–4, 11–12

Leighton, M. 48
liberalism 91–2, 115, 146n
love 23–4, 69–70

management 95–8, 120–1
marriage 51, 103–10, 111,
   113, 119, 124
martyrdom 25–9, 139
Marx, Karl 6
masculinity 109, 118–20
media 32, 116, 128, 139–40
Midgley, Mary 4
mobility 117–18
modernity 34, 35
Munton, Tony 117

nationalism 62–3, 65, 71–9
neo-conservatism 113–14
Nietzsche, Friedrich 6, 15–16

O'Connor, Fionnuala 76

Parliament 100–1
Paul, St 64–5
penal system 125–6
Phillips, Angela 118–19
Pope Pius XII 84
post-modernity 35
poverty 110–12, 121–4
progress 33

racism 80–2
rave culture 60–2, 69
relativism, moral Chapter 1
   passim, 137
religion 62–5, 68, 84–6; *see
   also* Christian ethics;
   education, and the churches
resurrection of Jesus 28–9, 70
rules, moral 3–4, 11–12, 43–4,
   131

scapegoating 79–80, 114, 126
Schluter, M. and Lee, D.
   117–18
Schumpeter, J. 137–8
science, natural 3, 11, 30–2,
   85–6
secularism 27, 85–6
self–fulfilment: Chapter 2
   passim, 52–3, 115–17; and
   suffering 23–9
selfishness 18–22
sex 58–60, 68
Shaffer, Peter 66–7, 69–70,
   77–8
single parenthood 106–7,
   108, 109
scepticism: moral 3–10;
   religious 27
Skidelsky, Robert 136–7,
   138–9
subjectivism, moral 3–4,
   11–14
subsidiarity 120

Taylor, Charles 43, 155n
Thatcher, M. 110

tradition 33–6
tribalism 61, 63–5, Chapter 6
   passim

unemployment 40, 46, 49,
   112–13, 119

vengeance 69–70, 77–8
violence 68–9
von Moltke, Helmut James
   25–6

welfare state 110, 113–14,
   123–4
White, T. H. 52–3
Winterson, Jeannette 23–4
work: 40, Chapter 4 *passim*,
   116–18, 119, 127–8; the
   fragility of human 54–6;
   see also labour

Yevtushenko, Yevgeni 83
youth culture 34–5, 116,
   156n

Zeldin, Theodore 87–8